Why Models Fail

A Quant's Guide to Overfitting and Signal Decay

Victor Trex

Published by NobleTrex Press

For permissions and other inquiries, write to:
P.O. Box 3132, Framingham, MA 01701, USA

Contents

Introduction

Quantitative models fail more often than they succeed-not because their creators lack ingenuity, but because markets are noisy, adaptive, and unforgiving of shortcuts. This book is about confronting that reality with rigor. It is a guide to recognizing when apparent skill is a statistical mirage, when validation is compromised by leakage, and when genuine edges inevitably decay under the pressure of competition, capacity, and changing regimes. Rather than offering another catalog of signals, we focus on the engineering, statistical, and governance practices that separate fragile backtests from robust, tradable systems.

Our premise is simple: if one searches long and hard enough in historical data, one will always find patterns. The question is whether those patterns survive out of sample, after costs, in size, and under drift. The first chapter, on statistical and mathematical foundations, equips you to answer that question with discipline. We revisit probability and inference with an eye toward noisy financial time series-where autocorrelation, heteroskedasticity, and asynchrony are the rule, not the exception. We link risk and performance metrics to their sampling error so that a Sharpe ratio is not merely a headline number but a distribution with uncertainty. And we outline how optimization and regularization control effective degrees of freedom, translating abstract bias-variance trade-offs into practical choices that tame search intensity.

Data is where many failures begin. The chapter on data integrity and leakage shows how illusory alpha is born from non-point-in-time inputs, survivorship bias, misapplied corporate actions, misaligned calendars, and subtle label leaks. We stress that a credible research environment reconstructs the information set exactly as it was known, at each timestamp, with complete auditability. Clean keys, revision-aware pipelines, and explicit universe rules are not administrative niceties; they are the scaffolding that prevents future information from seeping into the past.

Even with pristine data, models falter when validation is porous. The chapter on validation and robust backtesting presents time-aware splits, purged and embargoed partitions, and walk-forward protocols that respect dependence. We adapt cross-validation and resampling to block structure, and we treat multiple testing as a first-order concern. False discovery control, nested tuning, and lockboxes protect the final evaluation from becoming a moving target. Backtests are built to mirror tradable reality: point-in-time signals, realistic latency, parameter freezes, and explicit cost models turn optimism into tempered expectation.

Overfitting is not just a cautionary tale; it is a quantifiable process. In the chapter on overfitting theory and diagnostics, we connect model complexity, sample size, and search to variance inflation. Information criteria and minimum description length embed a preference for parsimony. We adjust headline performance using probabilistic and deflated Sharpe frameworks that account for non-normality and repeated trials. The probability of backtest overfitting becomes a diagnostic to estimate how often selection favored a fluke. These tools do not eliminate risk, but they sharpen our priors about what is likely to endure.

Real edges decay-even honest ones. The chapter on signal decay, regimes, and implementation frictions explains why. Concepts drift as participants learn, capital crowds in, and microstructure evolves. We measure persistence via half-life and stability diagnostics, detect structural breaks and change points, and condition evaluation on regimes. Portfolio construction transforms raw signals through scaling, constraints, and risk models, often diluting paper alpha while increasing turnover. Capacity limits, costs, and impact compress realized P&L long before theoretical limits are reached, and execution quality-order types, slippage, latency-ties statistical edge to market plumbing.

Finally, model failure is an operational risk to be governed, not a one-off embarrassment. The chapter on governance, monitoring, and lifecycle frames roles, policies, and challenge processes that institutionalize skepticism. Documentation, versioning, and pre-registration build a chain of custody from idea to production. Live-versus-backtest tracking, drift alerts, and KPI thresholds detect decay early, while champion-challenger workflows enable orderly refreshes and retirements. In this view, humility is not a personality trait; it is a control.

This text is intended for practitioners, students, and risk managers who want principled methods rather than folklore. We assume comfort with basic statistics, linear algebra, and programming, but we aim to make every concept operational and testable. Throughout, concise concept markers highlight core ideas and cross-references, and reproducible pipelines anchor the examples. Read linearly for a full treatment, or dip into the chapters that match the weakest links in your current process. Either way, the goal is the same: to turn alluring backtests into resilient strategies by insisting that evidence be earned, not inferred.

Chapter 1

Statistical and Mathematical Foundations

Most models don't fail because the math was wrong-they fail because the right math was never applied to the right questions. This chapter arms you with the core statistical and optimization tools needed to tell genuine signal from seductive noise, to understand what your backtests are really saying, and to recognize the early mathematical warning signs of a strategy that will not survive contact with live markets.

1.1 Probability and Inference Essentials

Most quantitative failures begin with a simple confusion: taking patterns produced by random noise and treating them as real, exploitable structure. To avoid that trap, we need a small but sharp toolkit from probability and statistics. In this section, we build that toolkit with one guiding question in mind:

> Given historical returns, how can we tell whether we are seeing a genuine trading edge or just a lucky draw from a noisy process?

We will proceed in four steps:

1. Model returns as random variables with specific distributions, paying special attention to tails.
2. Define expectations and variances so we can talk about "true" performance and risk.
3. Introduce estimators—sample mean, variance, regression coefficients—and their uncertainty.
4. Use hypothesis tests and confidence intervals to decide when a measured edge is statistically believable.

Throughout, the focus is not abstract mathematics but what these ideas mean for your backtests and live strategies.

Returns as Random Variables

From a modeling perspective, a one-period return is a random variable: before the period ends, we do not know its value, only the distribution of possible values. You can think of that distribution as a bag of numbers that nature draws from each period.

Two comments are crucial for quants:

- The distribution is about *population* behavior over many hypothetical realizations, not just the one time series we observed.
- The shape of the distribution—center, spread, skewness, tail thickness—determines both economic risk and how hard it is to estimate performance accurately.

Common Distributions for Returns

A few stylized distributions recur in quantitative finance models:

- **Normal (Gaussian).** Symmetric, bell-shaped, fully determined by its mean and variance. Convenient mathematically and often used as a first approximation. We write $R \sim N(\mu, \sigma^2)$.
- **Student-t.** Also symmetric with a peak around its center, but with heavier tails. Controlled by degrees of freedom ν. Lower ν means heavier tails and more extreme moves. Often used to capture "fat tails" in returns.
- **Bernoulli / Binary payoff.** Return takes one of two values, for example $+1\%$ with probability p and -1% with probability $1 - p$. Useful for modeling strategies that mostly earn small gains but occasionally lose.
- **Mixtures.** Combinations of simple distributions, for example "95% of the time returns are drawn from a low-volatility regime, 5% of the time from a crisis regime." Mixtures naturally produce heavy tails and regime shifts.

The choice of distribution is not just a convenience. It encodes your beliefs about how often extreme moves occur. Because estimation error grows rapidly with tail thickness, underestimating tails makes you overconfident in your backtests.

Normal vs Heavy-Tailed Returns

In textbooks, daily returns often appear close to normal: mostly small moves, occasional but not crazy large moves, symmetric around a modest mean. Real markets, however, produce more extreme events than a normal model suggests: crashes, sudden rallies, regime shifts.

One way to see the difference:

- Under a standard normal distribution, a 5σ event is extraordinarily rare.

- In real return series, events of that magnitude (relative to recent volatility) are far more common.

The Student-t distribution with low degrees of freedom mimics this behavior. It has the same basic shape as the normal in the center, but its tails decay more slowly. That means:

- More drawdowns than a normal model predicts.
- Sample moments (mean, variance) jump around more from sample to sample.
- Backtest performance is less stable, especially when your window is not very long.

The figure shows the key intuition: two return processes that look very similar near zero can have dramatically different probabilities of extreme moves. From a modeling perspective, those extreme moves are where your estimates of risk and performance become fragile.

Expectation, Variance, and Covariance

Once we have a distribution for returns, we can define basic population concepts that we will try to estimate from data.

Expectation: The Long-Run Average

The expectation (or mean) of a return R is its long-run average outcome if we could repeat the process indefinitely under identical conditions. For a simple discrete case,

$$\mathbb{E}[R] = \sum_i r_i\, p_i,$$

where r_i are possible returns and p_i their probabilities.

Intuitively, if a strategy has $\mathbb{E}[R] = 0.05\%$ per day, then over a very long horizon we expect it to earn about 0.05% per day on average, though any finite sample will fluctuate around that.

For a quant, the expectation is the "true edge." When we run a backtest and compute an average historical return, we are trying to infer this expectation from one finite path of data.

Variance and Standard Deviation: Dispersion Around the Mean

The variance of R measures how variable returns are around their mean. One common definition is

$$\mathrm{Var}(R) = \mathbb{E}[(R - \mathbb{E}[R])^2].$$

The square root of variance is the standard deviation. In practice, people often talk about "volatility" instead of standard deviation. Higher volatility means that:

- The strategy's realized path can deviate a lot from its mean.
- Short-term performance is dominated by noise rather than by edge.
- We need more data to estimate the mean with a given precision.

This last point is crucial: if your volatility is high relative to your expected return, you will need a very long sample to be confident that your positive backtest is not just luck.

Covariance and Correlation: Co-Movement

In multi-asset or multi-signal settings, we care not just about each return on its own but about how they move together. The covariance of two returns R and S is

$$\mathrm{Cov}(R, S) = \mathbb{E}[(R - \mathbb{E}[R])(S - \mathbb{E}[S])].$$

The correlation is a scaled version of covariance that lies between -1 and 1. Positive correlation means the two returns tend to be above or below their means at the same time; negative correlation means one tends to be up when the other is down.

Correlation matters for model failure in two ways:

- When you combine strategies, ignoring correlations leads to overestimation of diversification benefits.
- When you fit a model (such as a regression), collinearity among predictors (high correlations) can make parameter estimates unstable and sensitive to noise.

From Population to Sample: Estimators

In reality, we never see the full distribution. We only see a finite sample: a time series of returns, factor values, signals, and so on. To connect theoretical quantities (like $\mathbb{E}[R]$) to data, we use *estimators*.

Think of an estimator as a recipe that takes in your historical data and outputs a guess of some population quantity.

Sample Mean and Sampling Variability

Given returns $R_1, R_2, \ldots, R_T$, a natural estimator of the mean is the sample average:

$$\hat{\mu} = \frac{1}{T} \sum_{t=1}^{T} R_t.$$

Two important properties:

- On average, $\hat{\mu}$ is correct: if we could repeat the sample many times, the mean of all the $\hat{\mu}$'s would equal the true μ (under standard assumptions).
- For any *one* sample, $\hat{\mu}$ can be far from μ, especially when T is small or volatility is high.

The randomness of $\hat{\mu}$ across hypothetical repeated samples is called *sampling variability*. It is at the heart of overfitting: every time we try a new strategy, its estimated mean return is a random draw around its true mean, and we tend to notice and trade the lucky ones.

Bias, Variance, and Consistency

Three terms will recur throughout this book:

- **Bias.** The difference between the estimator's long-run average and the true parameter. An unbiased estimator has zero bias.
- **Variance of an estimator.** How much the estimator fluctuates from sample to sample.
- **Consistency.** An estimator is consistent if, as the sample size grows, it converges (in probability) to the true parameter.

In many financial problems, we are willing to accept a little bias (for example, by using a shrinkage estimator) if it significantly reduces variance, since high variance in parameters often translates into fragile portfolios or models that shift wildly over time.

Estimating Variance and Covariance

We can similarly estimate variance and covariance from data. The standard sample variance is

$$\hat{\sigma}^2 = \frac{1}{T-1} \sum_{t=1}^{T} (R_t - \hat{\mu})^2,$$

and the sample covariance between R and S is

$$\widehat{\text{Cov}}(R, S) = \frac{1}{T-1} \sum_{t=1}^{T} (R_t - \hat{\mu}_R)(S_t - \hat{\mu}_S).$$

These are again random quantities: each new sample of data will give slightly different $\hat{\sigma}^2$ and covariance estimates.

Why should a quant care?

- Portfolio optimization uses these as inputs. Estimation error in covariances often dominates everything else.
- Standard errors of performance metrics (Sharpe ratios, regression alphas) depend on volatility and covariances.
- In small samples, variance estimates can be very noisy, leading to overly levered or overly concentrated portfolios.

Regression Coefficients as Estimators

Much of quantitative modeling can be recast as regression. For example, suppose we model a strategy return R_t as

$$R_t = \alpha + \beta F_t + \varepsilon_t,$$

where F_t is a factor (say, the market), α is the strategy's edge beyond the factor, and β is its exposure.

The ordinary least squares (OLS) estimator produces $\hat{\alpha}$ and $\hat{\beta}$ from data by choosing values that minimize the sum of squared residuals. Again:

- $\hat{\alpha}$ and $\hat{\beta}$ are random variables across hypothetical samples.
- Their sampling variability is governed by the volatility of ε_t, the variability of F_t, and their sample size and correlation structure.

If you fit the same regression on two overlapping time windows and obtain very different $\hat{\alpha}$'s, that may be a sign that your edge is weak relative to noise or that market conditions have changed.

Standard Errors and Confidence Intervals

To move from point estimates to uncertainty quantification, we introduce *standard errors* and *confidence intervals.*

Standard Error: Typical Estimation Noise

The standard error of an estimator is the standard deviation of its sampling distribution: it measures how much the estimator would fluctuate if you could resample your data under the same conditions.

For the sample mean under simple assumptions (independent, identically distributed returns with variance σ^2), the standard error is approximately

$$\text{SE}(\hat{\mu}) \approx \frac{\sigma}{\sqrt{T}}.$$

This captures several intuitions:

- More data (T larger) reduces uncertainty.
- Higher volatility (σ larger) increases uncertainty about the mean.

In practice, we replace σ by the sample standard deviation. Similar formulas exist, with more caveats, for regression coefficients and other estimators.

Confidence Intervals: Ranges of Plausible Values

A confidence interval for a parameter (such as the mean return or alpha) is a range that, under the model assumptions, will contain the true value with a chosen long-run frequency (for example, 95%).

For a mean return with an approximately normal sampling distribution, a 95% confidence interval might look like

$$\hat{\mu} \pm 2 \times \text{SE}(\hat{\mu}).$$

Interpretation in the backtest context:

- If the entire interval lies above zero, your data are consistent with a positive true edge, assuming the model is correct.
- If the interval straddles zero, then the data are compatible with both positive and negative true means. You cannot rule out the possibility that you have no edge (or even a negative one), even if $\hat{\mu}$ itself is positive.

Confidence intervals are often more informative than point estimates, because they force you to confront how wide the range of plausible true performance really is.

Hypothesis Testing: Is This Edge Real?

Hypothesis testing formalizes the decision problem: given an observed estimate, should we treat the strategy's edge as statistically different from zero?

Null and Alternative Hypotheses

We start by defining:

- The *null hypothesis* H_0: typically "no edge." For a strategy's mean return, $H_0 : \mu = 0$.
- The *alternative hypothesis* H_1: the possibility we care about. For example, $H_1 : \mu > 0$ (a positive edge).

We then compute a test statistic that measures how far the estimated parameter is from what the null predicts, in units of its standard error. For a mean,

$$t = \frac{\hat{\mu} - 0}{\mathrm{SE}(\hat{\mu})}.$$

p-Values and Significance

The *p-value* is the probability, under the null hypothesis, of observing a test statistic as extreme as (or more extreme than) the one we got. A small p-value means that, if there really were no edge, it would be unusual to see such a large estimated mean.

Traditionally, people pick a significance level (for example, 5%) and reject the null if the p-value is below this threshold.

In trading terms:

- A small p-value suggests the observed Sharpe or alpha is unlikely to be pure noise, under the model used for the test.
- A large p-value suggests that the observed performance is quite compatible with zero true edge.

However, p-values come with important caveats, especially in the context of strategy discovery.

Effect Size, Power, and Multiple Testing

Three issues are particularly relevant to overfitting:

- **Effect size.** A statistically significant edge can still be economically tiny. For example, a very small positive mean return can be highly significant with enough data, yet irrelevant after costs and capacity constraints. Always look at both the magnitude of the effect and its statistical significance.
- **Power.** Power is the probability of correctly rejecting the null when a true edge exists. Low power means that even genuinely profitable strategies will often look insignificant in sample. Power increases with sample size, with the true effect size, and when noise (volatility) is lower.
- **Multiple testing and data snooping.** In research, you rarely test one strategy. You test hundreds or thousands of variations, consciously or unconsciously. Even if each test has a 5% false positive rate, the chance that *at least one* looks significant by luck alone becomes very high. This is one of the main mechanisms of overfitting: the more tests you run, the more likely you are to fool yourself with random winners.

Standard hypothesis tests and p-values assume that you decided on the strategy and test *before* looking at the data. Once you use the data to drive the search itself, classical p-values are no longer valid without adjustments.

In later chapters, we will discuss techniques to correct for multiple testing, such as Bonferroni adjustments, false discovery rate control, and resampling-based methods tailored to backtests. For now, the key takeaway is:

> A small p-value from a single test is weak evidence in a research process that has quietly tried many variations.

Interpreting Evidence of Edge

Putting these pieces together, how should a quant interpret the output of a backtest?

- Model your returns with a realistic distribution, acknowledging heavy tails and dependence where present. Do not rely purely on normal assumptions.
- Treat sample estimates (means, Sharpe, alpha) as noisy realizations of underlying parameters. Always ask: what is their standard error?
- Use confidence intervals to quantify the range of plausible true performance. Prefer statements like "the 95% confidence interval for annualized Sharpe is between 0.1 and 1.0" over "the Sharpe is 0.6."
- When testing for edge, define your null hypothesis explicitly and interpret p-values in the context of how many strategies and variations were tried.
- Distinguish statistical from economic significance. A small but statistically clear edge may or may not be tradable once costs, slippage, and capacity are considered.

These probability and inference tools do not guarantee that your models will be right. Markets change, and all models are simplifications. But they provide a disciplined language for quantifying uncertainty, for separating plausible edge from obvious noise, and for recognizing when apparent success is likely to be an artifact of overfitting.

In the next sections, we will move from single-period randomness to time-series structure, exploring how serial dependence, nonstationarity, and volatility dynamics further complicate—and sometimes invalidate—the simple i.i.d. framework used here.

1.2 Time-Series Dependence and Properties

In the previous section we treated returns mostly as independent draws from some distribution. That framework is useful for understanding noise, estimation error, and basic inference. Real financial data, however, arrive as *time series*: ordered sequences where today's value is connected to yesterday's and tomorrow's. Those connections—the time-series properties of the data—strongly constrain what we can safely infer from historical performance.

This section focuses on three themes:

- **Serial dependence**: how returns relate to their own past.
- **Nonstationarity**: how the statistical properties of returns can change over time.
- **Volatility dynamics**: how the variability of returns clusters and evolves.

Each of these complicates the simple "independent and identically distributed" (i.i.d.) picture and, if ignored, leads to overconfident backtests and fragile models.

From i.i.d. Draws to Time Series

A time series is an ordered collection of random variables, such as daily log-returns

$$R_1, R_2, \dots, R_T.$$

In the i.i.d. world, each R_t is drawn independently from the same distribution. That assumption underlies many textbook results: simple formulas for standard errors, classical hypothesis tests, and so on.

In financial data, three empirical regularities break the strict i.i.d. view:

- Returns may exhibit *serial correlation* (for example, trends or mean reversion).
- The distribution of returns may evolve (changes in mean, volatility, or higher moments).
- Volatility is clearly *time-varying* and tends to cluster in episodes of turbulence.

Each of these properties alters how much information your sample really contains. Ten years of highly autocorrelated data do not provide the same effective information as ten years of independent draws. Likewise, ten years that mix different regimes are not equivalent to ten years from one stable distribution.

Serial Dependence: Memory in Returns

Autocorrelation and Predictability

Serial dependence captures the idea that returns might be related to their own past. The simplest measure is the *autocorrelation* at lag k, which compares R_t with R_{t-k}.

Intuitively:

- A positive autocorrelation at lag 1 means that positive returns tend to be followed by positive returns, and negative by negative. This is trend-like behavior.
- A negative autocorrelation at lag 1 means that positive returns tend to be followed by negative returns and vice versa. This is mean-reverting behavior.
- Autocorrelations near zero suggest that returns are largely unpredictable at that horizon, at least linearly.

For example, suppose daily returns show almost no autocorrelation at lag 1, but weekly returns show positive autocorrelation at lag 1. This pattern is consistent with a momentum effect at the weekly horizon that is too weak to show up clearly day by day.

Random Walks and Martingale-Like Behavior

A *random walk* for prices is a simple model where the price today equals yesterday's price plus a random innovation:

$$P_t = P_{t-1} + \varepsilon_t,$$

with the ε_t's roughly independent, zero-mean shocks. In that case, returns (differences in price or log-price) are approximately independent over time, even though prices themselves are highly persistent.

This distinction is crucial:

- Prices can look extremely smooth and trending simply because they accumulate many small, independent shocks over time.
- Returns, not prices, are the objects in which we usually search for predictability and measure performance.

If you regress price on lagged price, you will almost always find a coefficient near one and a very high R^2. This does *not* imply predictable profits; it mostly reflects the mechanical accumulation of shocks in a random walk.

Mean Reversion and Trend Following

Some strategies rely explicitly on serial dependence:

- **Momentum / trend following** builds on positive autocorrelation: recent winners tend to keep winning for a while.
- **Statistical arbitrage / pairs trading** often relies on mean reversion: when a price or spread deviates too far from some reference level, it tends to move back.

If returns are truly independent over the relevant horizon, such strategies cannot generate a genuine edge purely from serial structure. Any apparent profitability would have to come from other sources (for example, compensation for risk or exposure to other factors) or from overfitting.

For a quant, the task is not just to detect autocorrelation but to judge whether it is large and stable enough, after costs, to translate into a robust signal.

Stationarity: Are the Rules of the Game Constant?

Weak Stationarity

A time series is called *weakly stationary* if its mean, variance, and autocovariances do not depend on time. Informally, the process follows the same statistical rules throughout the sample. The distribution might be non-normal, but its shape and dependencies are stable.

Most classical inference tools implicitly assume some form of stationarity:

- When you compute an average over the whole sample and treat it as a meaningful estimate of the "true" mean, you are assuming the mean has not shifted.
- When you estimate a single volatility or autocorrelation over the whole sample, you are assuming those features are constant.

In reality, markets evolve. Trading rules, regulation, technology, and participant behavior all change, sometimes suddenly. We observe:

- Long stretches of low volatility followed by turbulent periods.
- Regime shifts in average returns after structural breaks (for example, policy changes).
- Changes in the strength or even the sign of correlations between assets or factors.

Strict stationarity is more a benchmark than a description of reality, but it is a useful benchmark because it clarifies when our usual formulas become suspect.

Nonstationarity and Regime Shifts

Nonstationarity simply means that some aspect of the distribution changes over time. This can take several forms:

- **Drifting mean**: the unconditional average return changes (for example, before and after a major crisis).
- **Changing volatility**: variance rises or falls over time, possibly in persistent episodes.
- **Shifting correlation structure**: relationships among assets or factors strengthen, weaken, or reverse.

From a model failure perspective, nonstationarity is dangerous because:

- A backtest that mixes multiple regimes may produce an average performance figure that matches none of them.
- An edge that existed in an earlier regime may have decayed or disappeared by the end of the backtest, yet the average still looks attractive.
- Parameters calibrated on past data may be systematically biased when applied to a new regime.

One practical response is to place more weight on recent data when fitting models, or to explicitly detect and model regime changes. However, overreacting to short-term changes can itself cause overfitting. There is no free lunch: handling nonstationarity is about making informed trade-offs between stability and adaptability.

Volatility Clustering and Conditional Heteroskedasticity

What Volatility Clustering Looks Like

If you plot returns over time, you rarely see isolated spikes of volatility evenly sprinkled across the sample. Instead, you see *volatility clustering*: periods where returns are relatively calm alternate with periods where they are consistently more turbulent.

Two empirical facts stand out:

- Raw returns often have little autocorrelation, but *squared* or *absolute* returns show strong serial dependence.
- High-volatility periods tend to follow each other, and shocks to volatility decay slowly.

This pattern is called *conditional heteroskedasticity*: the variance of returns conditional on recent information changes over time. Models such as GARCH are designed to capture this feature.

Why Volatility Dynamics Matter for Inference

Ignoring volatility clustering leads to several problems:

- Standard errors based on constant-variance assumptions will typically be biased downward, making you overconfident about estimated means, Sharpe ratios, and alphas.
- Backtests that happen to start in a low-volatility environment and end in a high-volatility one (or vice versa) can misrepresent the typical risk experienced by an investor.
- Risk controls calibrated on a benign period will fail during clustered volatility episodes, where losses arrive in rapid succession.

In short, volatility dynamics shrink the effective amount of independent information in your sample. Ten years of data that consist mostly of a single, long high-volatility episode provide less information about typical behavior than ten years composed of many independent episodes.

Autocorrelation Functions and Diagnostic Tools

To study serial dependence and volatility clustering in practice, we use simple diagnostic tools such as the *autocorrelation function* (ACF).

- The ACF of returns at various lags reveals linear predictability in the mean.
- The ACF of squared or absolute returns reveals persistence in volatility.

For example, you may find that daily returns have near-zero autocorrelation at all lags (efficient in the mean), but squared returns have positive autocorrelation that decays slowly (persistent volatility).

Practical Complications for Backtesting

Time-series properties do not just affect abstract theory; they alter how you must design and interpret backtests.

Overlapping Returns and Effective Sample Size

Many strategies operate on horizons longer than a single observation period. For example, you might examine one-month holding-period returns computed daily. These returns overlap in time: the return from day 1 to day 21 shares almost all its components with the return from day 2 to day 22.

Overlapping returns create artificial serial correlation even if underlying daily returns are independent. This reduces the *effective* number of independent observations. Naively plugging the raw count of observations into standard error formulas will make you think you have more information than you really do.

In practice:

- Be cautious when using overlapping windows to evaluate long-horizon strategies.
- Use methods that adjust for overlapping data when computing standard errors.

Look-Ahead Bias and Time Alignment

Time-series dependence also means that errors in time alignment can create spurious predictability. If a signal at time t inadvertently incorporates information only available at time $t + 1$, you introduce *look-ahead bias*. The backtest will appear to predict the future, but only because it is allowed to cheat.

Examples include:

- Using revised or restated economic data as if it were available in real time.

- Using end-of-day prices to compute signals that are then assumed to trade at that same close.
- Mishandling corporate actions such as dividends or splits in a way that leaks future information.

Given serial dependence, even small time shifts can produce large artificial edges. Rigorous time-stamping and alignment of all series in a backtest are therefore essential.

Sampling Frequency and Apparent Predictability

How often you sample prices and compute returns affects observed time-series properties:

- At very high frequencies, microstructure effects (bid-ask bounce, latency, order book dynamics) dominate, often causing negative autocorrelation in returns.
- At intermediate frequencies (say, daily to weekly), many assets show near-zero autocorrelation in raw returns but strong dependence in volatility.
- At lower frequencies (monthly or longer), macroeconomic and behavioral phenomena may create more visible trends or mean reversion.

A strategy that looks predictive at one sampling frequency may not survive transaction costs, slippage, and capacity constraints at the trading frequency it requires. Conversely, an effect that is invisible at the daily level might become clear when aggregated to monthly horizons.

When you change sampling frequency, you change both the economic meaning of your signal and the statistical properties of the returns. Inference must be reconsidered accordingly.

Time-Aware Validation and Overfitting Risk

Train/Test Splits Must Respect Time

Standard cross-validation in machine learning often shuffles observations or uses random folds. In time series, this destroys temporal structure and can leak information from the future into the past.

For backtests and forecasting models, you should:

- Split data into training and testing based on time, not at random.
- Use rolling or expanding windows that mimic real-time model updating.
- Ensure that each evaluation period uses parameter estimates that only rely on past data.

Ignoring these principles leads to validation procedures that dramatically understate overfitting risk.

Dependence and the Illusion of Many Observations

Serial dependence reduces the amount of independent information in your sample. For example, if daily returns are strongly autocorrelated, then 250 daily observations contain much less independent information than 250 draws from an i.i.d. process.

This has two key implications:

- Standard formulas for p-values and confidence intervals that assume independence will be too optimistic.
- A search over many features or signals in a time series with strong dependence will produce more apparent patterns than truly exist, increasing the risk of data-snooping and overfitting.

In later chapters, we will exploit block-bootstrap and other dependence-aware resampling methods to better quantify uncertainty in backtests. For now, recognize that dependence magnifies the risk that a pattern you discover is merely a byproduct of sampling noise plus temporal structure.

What Time-Series Properties Allow—and Forbid

Time-series dependence, nonstationarity, and volatility dynamics do not make quantitative modeling impossible, but they sharply constrain what you can reasonably infer from historical data.

- If returns are nearly serially uncorrelated at your trading horizon, then any model claiming strong short-term predictability is suspect unless it has a very compelling economic rationale and careful treatment of costs.
- Nonstationarity means that even genuine past edges may not persist. Average performance over long windows can hide important regime changes.
- Volatility clustering implies that risk is more unstable than naive models assume. Strategies that look safe in quiet periods can become dangerously leveraged in turbulent regimes.
- Time-series dependence reduces effective sample size. Apparent significance based on naive formulas often overstates the evidence for edge.

The purpose of this section has been to shift your mindset from seeing historical data as a large pile of independent evidence to seeing it as one particular path of a dependent, evolving process. In the next section, we translate these time-series insights into the language of risk and performance metrics, examining how serial dependence and changing volatility distort Sharpe ratios, alphas, and drawdowns—and how that distortion leads directly to model failure when it is ignored.

1.3 Risk and Performance Metrics

Up to this point we have focused on two ingredients of quantitative work:

- The *distribution* of returns and the uncertainty in our estimates of its parameters.
- The *time-series structure* of returns, including dependence and changing volatility.

We now translate those ideas into the language quants use every day to judge strategies: Sharpe ratios, alphas, drawdowns, hit rates, and related statistics. These metrics are compact summaries of risk and reward, but they are also *estimators*: noisy functions of finite data. Misunderstanding their sampling error is one of the fastest routes to overfitting.

This section has four goals:

- Define core performance and risk measures in intuitive terms.
- Show how they relate to simple return distributions and time-series assumptions.
- Explain how unstable these measures can be in finite samples, especially with dependence and non-normality.
- Contrast statistical and economic significance, and how optimizing the wrong metric can systematically mislead you.

Return, Risk, and the Sharpe Ratio

Average Return and Volatility

Consider a single strategy with returns $R_1, \ldots, R_T$ over T periods, and let r_f denote the risk-free rate per period (which may be near zero at short horizons). We define:

- The *excess return* in period t as $X_t = R_t - r_f$.
- The sample mean excess return as the average of X_t across the sample.
- The sample volatility as the standard deviation of X_t.

Economically, the mean excess return is your average reward above a safe asset; volatility measures the typical size of fluctuations around that mean. Both are properties of the underlying return distribution, estimated from the data.

Sharpe Ratio: Reward per Unit of Risk

The *Sharpe ratio* is the most widely used summary of risk-adjusted performance. For a single strategy, the *true* Sharpe ratio is:

$$\text{Sharpe} = \frac{\mathbb{E}[X_t]}{\sqrt{\text{Var}(X_t)}}.$$

In words: long-run average excess return divided by long-run volatility. In practice, we only observe a finite sample, so we compute the *sample Sharpe* by replacing the true mean and volatility with their sample estimates.

Why do quants love Sharpe?

- It is dimensionless; a daily Sharpe of 1, once rescaled appropriately, is comparable to a monthly Sharpe of 1.
- Under a simple model with normal, i.i.d. returns, maximizing Sharpe coincides with maximizing expected utility for a risk-averse investor with quadratic utility.
- It provides a quick sense of how much "signal" (average return) you are getting per unit of "noise" (volatility).

However, the Sharpe ratio is not a fixed property of a strategy in the way mass is a property of an object. It is an *estimate* based on one historical path, and that estimate can vary a lot.

Sampling Error of Sharpe

Under the benchmark of independent, normal returns, the sampling distribution of the Sharpe ratio is approximately normal when T is large. A simple approximation for the standard error of the annualized Sharpe is:

$$\text{SE}(\widehat{\text{Sharpe}}) \approx \frac{1}{\sqrt{T}},$$

where T is measured in years of data. This is a rough rule of thumb, but it highlights two important points:

- With 1 year of data, the standard error of the Sharpe is roughly 1. A measured Sharpe of 1 does not tell you much; the true Sharpe could plausibly be negative or very positive.
- Even with 10 years of data, the standard error is about 0.3. A reported Sharpe of 1.0 with 10 years of data might correspond to a true Sharpe of 0.4 or 1.6.

Serial correlation and heavy tails both *increase* the standard error relative to this simple formula, making real-world Sharpe estimates even less precise. When you see a backtest claiming a Sharpe of 1.5 from two or three years of daily data, it is safer to think "statistically compatible with a wide range of true Sharpes, including much lower values" unless there is strong additional evidence.

Information Ratio, Alpha, and Beta

Sharpe compares a strategy to the risk-free asset. Often we care about performance *relative to a benchmark* or relative to systematic factors.

Information Ratio

Suppose you manage an active portfolio whose benchmark is an index with return B_t. The *active return* is $A_t = R_t - B_t$. The *information ratio* is:

$$\mathrm{IR} = \frac{\mathbb{E}[A_t]}{\sqrt{\mathrm{Var}(A_t)}},$$

estimated in practice from sample means and standard deviations. It measures how much value you add per unit of active risk. A low-volatility strategy that tracks the benchmark but adds a small, steady excess return can have a high information ratio.

From an inference perspective, the estimation issues are almost identical to Sharpe: we are still measuring a signal (average active return) over noise (active volatility), and the standard error shrinks slowly with sample size and is worsened by autocorrelation and fat tails.

Alpha and Beta in a Factor Model

Consider a simple regression of strategy returns on a benchmark or factor:

$$R_t = \alpha + \beta F_t + \varepsilon_t,$$

where F_t might be the market excess return or some other systematic factor. Here:

- β measures how sensitive the strategy is to the factor.
- α measures the average return after accounting for exposure to F_t.

In this setup:

- *Beta* is a risk measure: it captures systematic co-movement with the factor.
- *Alpha* is a performance measure: the intercept term is interpreted as "true skill" or edge beyond factor exposure.

Again, we only ever see estimates $\hat{\alpha}$ and $\hat{\beta}$. They are random variables across samples, with standard errors derived from regression theory. Under the usual assumptions:

- The standard error of $\hat{\alpha}$ shrinks roughly like $1/\sqrt{T}$, scaled by the volatility of regression residuals.
- Serial correlation or conditional heteroskedasticity in ε_t inflates that standard error.

From a model failure perspective, over-interpreting a noisy $\hat{\alpha}$ is a common error. Even if the true alpha is zero, some strategies will show positive estimated alphas purely by chance, especially if you test many strategies.

Testing Whether Alpha Is Different from Zero

Formally, you might test the null hypothesis $H_0 : \alpha = 0$ against $H_1 : \alpha > 0$. You compute a t-statistic:

$$t = \frac{\hat{\alpha}}{\mathrm{SE}(\hat{\alpha})}.$$

A large t-statistic (say, above 2 or 3 in absolute value) suggests that the observed alpha is unlikely under the null of no skill, *assuming* the regression assumptions hold and that you have not tested many strategies and reported only the best.

In practice:

- Time-series dependence in residuals and factor returns means the textbook regression standard errors are often too small unless you adjust them.
- Multiple testing across strategies or factor combinations means the effective "surprise" in a large t-statistic is much smaller than the nominal p-value would suggest.

The upshot is that alphas which look statistically impressive in a single regression can be much less convincing when viewed through the lens of a realistic research process.

Downside Risk: Drawdowns and Asymmetry

Sharpe, information ratio, and alpha treat upside and downside deviations from the mean symmetrically. Investors typically do not. They care more about large losses and sustained drawdowns than about occasional upside surprises.

Drawdown and Maximum Drawdown

A *drawdown* is the percentage drop from a running peak in the cumulative return or equity curve. If your strategy starts at 100, rises to 120, then falls to 90, the drawdown from the peak is $(90-120)/120 = -25\%$. The *maximum drawdown* (MaxDD) over a period is the largest such peak-to-trough decline.

Drawdown statistics capture aspects of risk that volatility misses:

- They account for the order of returns: clustering of losses matters.

- They are directly tied to investor experience: deep or prolonged drawdowns can cause clients (or yourself) to abandon the strategy.

However, MaxDD is a highly variable statistic in finite samples. For a given underlying process, different realized paths can produce very different maximum drawdowns:

- Two strategies with identical Sharpe ratios and identical return distributions can nonetheless show quite different drawdowns over a five-year window.
- Conversely, a strategy with modest Sharpe can get "lucky" and exhibit a benign drawdown profile in a backtest.

This variability makes it dangerous to treat a single realized maximum drawdown as a stable property of the strategy. Better practice is to use simulations or resampling—consistent with the time-series structure of returns—to estimate a distribution of possible drawdowns and quantify the uncertainty.

Sortino Ratio and Downside-Focused Metrics

To reflect asymmetric preferences, analysts sometimes replace total volatility in the Sharpe ratio with a measure of downside variability. The *Sortino ratio* is one example:

$$\text{Sortino} = \frac{\mathbb{E}[R_t - r_f]}{\sqrt{\mathbb{E}[\min(R_t - r_f, 0)^2]}},$$

where the denominator is the standard deviation of negative excess returns only.

In theory, this better reflects investors who are primarily concerned with downside deviations. In practice:

- Estimating downside volatility reliably requires enough observations of negative returns; in small samples, this can be very noisy.
- Heavy tails and volatility clustering make the realized downside behavior highly sample-dependent.

As with Sharpe, any downside-focused metric must be interpreted together with its sampling error and with awareness of the underlying return dynamics.

Hit Rate and Payoff Asymmetry

Two further descriptive statistics are often useful:

- *Hit rate*: the fraction of periods with positive returns.
- *Average gain vs average loss*: the typical size of positive and negative returns.

Strategies with low hit rates but large wins when they are right (for example, trend-followers) feel very different from strategies with high hit rates but occasional large losses (for example, many carry or short-volatility trades).

Although these are simple counts and averages, they are still estimators. A 60% hit rate over 50 trades is much less informative than 60% over 5,000 trades. And payoff asymmetry is especially sensitive to a few extreme observations, which means heavy tails and volatility clustering can distort the picture within limited samples.

From Point Estimates to Ranges: Confidence in Metrics

The central lesson from earlier sections is that any statistic computed from finite, dependent, heavy-tailed data is uncertain. Risk and performance metrics are no exception.

Confidence Intervals for Sharpe and Alpha

In principle, you can construct confidence intervals for Sharpe ratios and alphas:

- For Sharpe, use approximations based on its sampling distribution, adjusted for serial correlation if needed.
- For alpha, use regression-based standard errors, again adjusted for time-series dependence.

Instead of saying "our annualized Sharpe is 1.2", you might say "our best estimate of the annualized Sharpe is 1.2, with a 95% confidence interval from 0.4 to 2.0 under our model assumptions." The latter statement surfaces how fragile the conclusion may be.

In practice, constructing accurate intervals under realistic conditions can be complex, but even approximate ranges are better than ignoring uncertainty altogether.

Impact of Serial Correlation and Nonstationarity

Time-series dependence and changing volatility affect metrics in two ways:

- They directly change the economic meaning of a given Sharpe or alpha. For example, a strategy with the same Sharpe but higher serial correlation will tend to have deeper drawdowns.
- They invalidate naive standard error formulas that assume independent, identically distributed returns, leading to underestimation of uncertainty.

For instance, suppose a strategy's daily returns have positive autocorrelation. If you annualize daily Sharpe by simply multiplying by the square root of 252, you will overstate its annual Sharpe. Proper annualization in the presence of serial correlation requires adjusting for the autocorrelation structure.

Similarly, if the strategy's volatility doubled halfway through the sample, a single estimate of annualized volatility is averaging across two very different regimes. That affects not only Sharpe but any metric that relies on variance or higher moments.

Statistical vs Economic Significance

All of the metrics discussed so far can be analyzed statistically: we can ask whether they are significantly different from zero or from some benchmark value. But statistical significance is not the same as economic value.

Tiny but Significant vs Large but Noisy

With enough data, even a very small true edge can produce a highly significant estimated Sharpe or alpha. Conversely, with short samples and high volatility, a genuinely large edge may not reach traditional significance thresholds.

For example:

- A factor with a true annualized Sharpe of 0.3, traded at huge scale with low costs, could be economically compelling for a large institution. Yet detecting it statistically may require decades of data.
- A niche strategy with a backtested Sharpe of 2.0 over three years could be statistically compatible with a much lower true Sharpe once sampling error, serial correlation, and data-snooping are considered. Its real economic value may be modest or negative after capacity and costs.

Thus, you must always interpret p-values and t-statistics in the context of trading frictions, leverage constraints, and capital size.

Multiple Testing and Optimizing on Metrics

In research, you rarely compute one Sharpe ratio or alpha. You compute thousands across strategies, parameter sets, universes, and variations. You then tend to focus on those with the highest metrics.

This process has two consequences:

- The highest Sharpe or alpha in your backtest universe is almost certainly upward biased relative to its true value, even if *none* of the strategies has any real edge. You have simply selected the luckiest realizations.
- The metric itself becomes an optimization target. If you search over models to maximize in-sample Sharpe, you are actively overfitting to noise in that metric unless you use out-of-sample procedures or strong regularization.

The more flexible the model space and the looser the validation, the more extreme this bias becomes. In later chapters, we will discuss corrections for multiple testing and robust validation schemes. At this stage, the key point is that performance metrics are not just descriptive; they are often *objective functions* in an optimization, and this makes their sampling noise directly dangerous.

Metric Choice as a Modeling Decision

Finally, choosing which performance and risk metrics to emphasize is itself a modeling decision that shapes which strategies you will eventually trade.

Aligning Metrics with Investor Objectives

Different investors care about different features:

- A high-frequency desk may prioritize information ratio and capacity at low volatility.
- A macro fund may tolerate larger drawdowns in exchange for crisis performance.
- A retail-oriented product may need to limit drawdowns and volatility of returns more tightly than an institutional fund.

Optimizing for a single number—say, maximizing Sharpe—implicitly encodes a risk preference. If that preference does not match your true objective, your optimization will steer you towards strategies that look great on paper but are fragile in practice.

Examples of Misalignment and Overfitting

Common failure modes include:

- **Ignoring drawdowns**: A strategy optimized purely for Sharpe may achieve that by taking small, frequent profits and occasional huge losses. The backtest window may not contain a full realization of those losses, leading to a pleasant-looking equity curve and a time bomb in live trading.
- **Ignoring turnover and costs**: A model that maximizes in-sample Sharpe without an explicit transaction cost penalty will often trade excessively. The reported Sharpe, computed before realistic costs, overstates the true, implementable performance.

- **Ignoring capacity**: Strategies found by maximizing per-dollar Sharpe in backtests may rely on trades that do not scale. The realized performance at deployable capital may be much lower.

A more robust approach is to use a small set of complementary metrics—for example, Sharpe or information ratio, maximum drawdown, and turnover—and to treat them jointly, rather than chasing the optimum of a single one. This acts as a form of regularization: it prevents models from exploiting narrow features of the data that improve one metric at the cost of others.

Summary: Metrics as Noisy Lenses on Reality

Risk and performance metrics are indispensable. They condense long histories of returns into digestible numbers that guide research, risk management, and communication with stakeholders. But they are also noisy, path-dependent estimators tied to specific assumptions about distributions and time-series behavior.

For a quant concerned with overfitting and signal decay, three principles are essential:

- Treat every reported Sharpe, alpha, drawdown, and hit rate as a random variable with a sampling distribution, not as a fact.
- Always ask how time-series dependence, heavy tails, and nonstationarity may have distorted both the level of the metric and your estimate of its uncertainty.
- Choose and interpret metrics in light of economic realities: costs, capacity, leverage, and investor preferences.

In the next section, we will turn to the optimization machinery that takes these metrics—often as objectives or constraints—and translates them into concrete portfolios and model parameters. We will see how unconstrained optimization over noisy metrics amplifies overfitting, and how regularization can be used to tame that amplification.

1.4 Optimization and Regularization Primer

In the previous sections we built three pillars:

- A probabilistic view of returns and sampling error.
- An understanding of time-series dependence and nonstationarity.
- A language of risk and performance metrics: Sharpe, alpha, drawdowns, and so on.

We now turn to the machinery that turns all of this into concrete decisions: *optimization*. Whenever you fit a model or build a portfolio, you are solving an optimization problem, explicitly or implicitly. This section explains:

- How data and assumptions become an objective function and constraints.
- How optimization can amplify noise and create overfit solutions.
- How *regularization*—deliberately penalizing complexity or instability—helps control that overfitting.

From Data to Optimization Problems

Every quantitative model sits on the same conceptual pipeline:

- You observe historical data: returns, prices, signals, factors.
- You make assumptions about how those data were generated (distributions, dependencies, regimes).
- You choose a performance or likelihood criterion: Sharpe, alpha, tracking error, log-likelihood, utility.
- You choose constraints: budget, leverage limits, position bounds, turnover caps, risk limits.

- You feed all of this into an optimization algorithm, which returns parameters or portfolio weights.

Formally, you are choosing a vector of parameters θ (regression coefficients, portfolio weights, model hyperparameters) to optimize some objective function $J(\theta)$ subject to constraints $C(\theta) \leq 0$.

Model Fitting as Optimization

When you fit a linear regression of returns on signals, you are solving:

$$\min_{\beta} \sum_{t=1}^{T} (R_t - X_t^\top \beta)^2,$$

where X_t is a vector of signals and β the coefficients. This is *least squares*: choose coefficients that minimize the sum of squared residuals.

In likelihood-based models, you choose parameters θ to *maximize* the likelihood of observing the data under your model:

$$\max_{\theta} \mathcal{L}(\theta; \text{data}) \quad \text{or equivalently} \quad \max_{\theta} \log \mathcal{L}(\theta; \text{data}).$$

In both cases, you are asking: among all possible parameter values, which ones best "explain" the sample we observed?

Portfolio Construction as Optimization

In portfolio problems, your decision variable is typically a vector of weights w over assets or strategies. A classical mean–variance portfolio problem looks like:

$$\max_{w} w^\top \mu - \frac{\gamma}{2} w^\top \Sigma w$$

$$\text{subject to} \sum_i w_i = 1, \quad w_i \text{ within bounds, risk limits, etc.}$$

Here μ is the vector of expected excess returns, Σ is the covariance matrix of returns, and γ is a risk-aversion parameter. Again, we are using estimates of μ and Σ from data; the optimizer picks weights that balance return and risk as encoded by this objective.

The key idea is that in both model fitting and portfolio construction, *small* changes in estimated inputs can lead to *large* changes in the optimizer's output. This sensitivity is the channel through which estimation noise is turned into overfitting.

A Conceptual Diagram of the Optimization Pipeline

To keep the big picture in view, it is helpful to visualize the flow from data and assumptions to final parameters and portfolios. The diagram below emphasizes where regularization enters the pipeline.

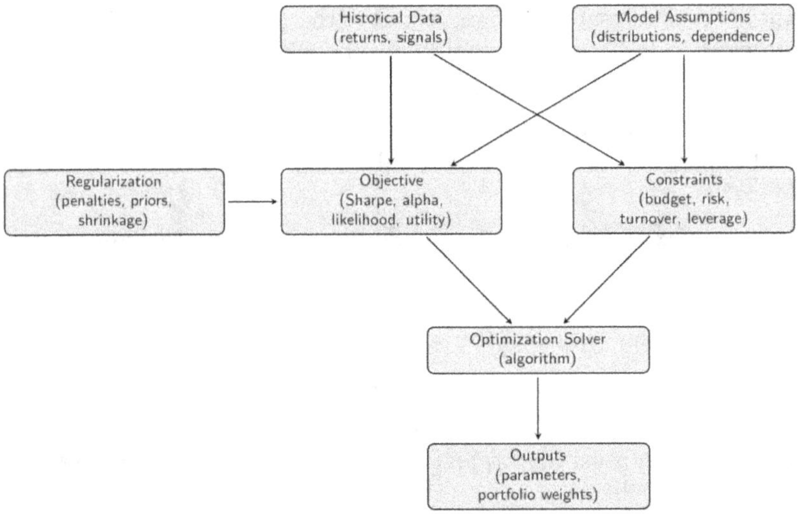

This flowchart highlights three levers you control:

- The **objective**: what you are trying to optimize.
- The **constraints**: what is allowed or forbidden.
- The **regularization**: extra terms or priors that penalize complexity or instability.

Overfitting arises when the combination of noisy inputs and an aggressive objective leads the solver to exploit patterns that are mostly noise. Regularization modifies the objective or constraints so that noisy patterns are less attractive.

Ill-Conditioning and Sensitivity to Noise

Optimization is most dangerous when the problem is *ill-conditioned*: small perturbations of inputs produce large changes in the optimal solution.

Examples of Ill-Conditioning

Two common sources in finance are:

- Highly correlated predictors or assets. In regression, if two signals are almost linear combinations of each other, many different coefficient vectors produce very similar fitted values. In portfolios, if two assets are nearly identical, there are many weight vectors that deliver almost the same risk and return.
- Noisy estimates of expected returns. Expected returns are notoriously hard to estimate. If you plug slightly different μ vectors into a mean–variance optimizer, you can get wildly different weight vectors, even when the underlying economic reality has not changed.

In such settings, the optimizer has many nearly equivalent solutions to choose from. Estimation noise nudges it toward one extreme or another, often resulting in:

- Concentrated positions in a few assets or signals.
- Large long/short positions that nearly cancel out but are highly sensitive to small return changes.
- Parameter values that jump around dramatically when you refit on slightly different data windows.

This is optimization *amplifying* noise. A weak underlying edge, or no edge at all, can be made to look strong in-sample by choosing extreme parameters that accidentally line up with random fluctuations.

The Bias–Variance Trade-Off

To understand why regularization helps, recall the concepts of *bias* and *variance* from earlier sections.

- **Bias** measures how far, on average, your estimator is from the true parameter.
- **Variance** measures how much your estimator fluctuates from sample to sample.

Unconstrained optimization typically aims for low bias: pick the parameters that fit the historical data best under your model. But when data are noisy and complex, this leads to high variance: the optimal parameters change a lot across samples.

Regularization deliberately introduces some bias to reduce variance:

- You restrict the class of models (for example, by penalizing large coefficients).
- You shrink estimates toward safer or more stable structures (for example, toward equal weights or a benchmark portfolio).

The goal is not to chase the best in-sample fit but to improve *out-of-sample* performance by choosing solutions that are less sensitive to noise.

Regularization in Regression: Ridge and Lasso

Consider again a linear model for returns:

$$R_t = X_t^\top \beta + \varepsilon_t,$$

where X_t is a vector of predictors. Ordinary least squares (OLS) chooses β to minimize the sum of squared residuals. Two classical regularization techniques modify this objective.

Ridge (L2) Regularization

Ridge regression adds an L2 penalty on the size of coefficients:

$$\min_{\beta} \sum_{t=1}^{T} (R_t - X_t^\top \beta)^2 + \lambda \sum_{j} \beta_j^2,$$

where $\lambda \geq 0$ controls the strength of the penalty.

Intuition:

- Large values of λ discourage large coefficients; all coefficients are shrunk toward zero.
- When predictors are highly correlated, ridge tends to distribute weight more evenly among them, rather than letting one coefficient become huge in magnitude to exploit small differences in the data.
- This reduces variance of the estimates and usually leads to better stability across time.

From an overfitting perspective, ridge prevents the optimizer from betting heavily on any one signal based solely on a noisy in-sample relationship.

Lasso (L1) Regularization

The lasso uses an L1 penalty:

$$\min_{\beta} \sum_{t=1}^{T} (R_t - X_t^\top \beta)^2 + \lambda \sum_{j} |\beta_j|.$$

The L1 penalty has a different effect:

- It encourages *sparse* solutions: many coefficients are driven exactly to zero.
- It performs implicit variable selection, choosing a subset of predictive signals and discarding the rest.

For quants, this is attractive when you start with a large menu of candidate signals. A lasso-style regularization can select a core subset while penalizing complexity. But, as always, the choice of λ is crucial: too small and you get little regularization; too large and you throw away useful signals.

Regularization in Portfolios: Shrinkage and Constraints

Regularization also plays a central role in portfolio construction.

Shrinkage Toward a Benchmark

One simple and effective idea is to *shrink* the optimal portfolio toward a benchmark or simple structure. For example, suppose w^* is the unconstrained mean–variance optimal portfolio based on your estimates of μ and Σ, and w^{bench} is a benchmark, such as:

- The market-cap weighted index.
- The equal-weight portfolio.
- A simple risk-parity portfolio.

A shrinkage approach sets the final portfolio to:

$$\tilde{w} = (1 - \alpha)w^{bench} + \alpha w^*,$$

for some α between 0 and 1. Here:

- $\alpha = 1$ corresponds to fully trusting the optimizer.
- $\alpha = 0$ corresponds to fully ignoring it and holding the benchmark.

Intermediate values trade off between potential alpha and stability. Shrinkage acts as regularization by limiting the optimizer's ability to exploit fragile aspects of the estimated inputs. It is equivalent to adding a penalty on deviation from the benchmark to the objective function.

Penalizing Turnover and Transaction Costs

Another powerful regularizer in practice is a turnover or transaction cost penalty. Instead of maximizing expected return minus a risk penalty, you maximize:

$$\text{expected performance} - \text{risk penalty} - \text{trading cost penalty}.$$

The trading cost penalty might be proportional to the absolute change in positions or use a more sophisticated nonlinear model. Economically, this captures the reality that every trade has a cost.

Statistically, it also regularizes the optimizer:

- It discourages rapid, high-amplitude changes in weights driven by small updates in estimated parameters.
- It smooths the portfolio path through time, reducing variance in realized performance and mitigating the impact of short-lived in-sample patterns.

Without such penalties, an optimizer armed with a noisy signal of expected returns will tend to trade excessively, chasing every wiggle in the estimated edge.

Position and Risk Constraints as Regularization

Constraints that might appear purely practical also have a regularizing effect. Examples include:

- Limits on individual position sizes or sector exposures.
- Constraints on gross leverage or net exposure.
- Bounds on portfolio volatility or tracking error.

By restricting the solution space, these constraints:

- Prevent the optimizer from choosing extreme, fragile portfolios that happen to look good in-sample.
- Force diversification across assets, factors, or styles.

In this sense, risk management constraints are a form of structural regularization: they codify prior beliefs about what kinds of portfolios are acceptable and prevent overfitting from driving you far from those priors.

Choosing the Strength of Regularization

A key practical question is: how much regularization is enough?

Cross-Validation and Out-of-Sample Tests

One principled approach is to treat the regularization strength (for example, λ in ridge/lasso or α in shrinkage) as a hyperparameter and choose it using:

- **Out-of-sample backtests**: fit models on earlier data with different levels of regularization and evaluate performance on later periods.
- **Time-series cross-validation**: rolling or expanding windows that respect temporal order and measure how different regularization levels affect predictive performance.

You are then trading off in-sample fit against out-of-sample robustness. Too little regularization yields high apparent in-sample performance and poor stability; too much regularization yields dull but robust performance that may underuse genuine signals.

Economic Priors

Another approach is to encode economic beliefs directly:

- If you believe that true signals are small and sparse, you might favor stronger L1 regularization.
- If you believe that long/short position sizes should be limited by liquidity and risk appetite, you might set tight position and leverage constraints.
- If you believe that trading costs are substantial, you might impose a strong turnover penalty even if out-of-sample backtests on frictionless data suggest more frequent trading.

These economic priors help prevent purely statistical tuning from pushing regularization too low, especially in settings with multiple testing and data-snooping risks.

Optimization as an Amplifier of Overfitting

Bringing the themes together:

- Historical data provide noisy estimates of return distributions and time-series properties.
- Performance metrics like Sharpe and alpha are noisy functions of those estimates.
- Optimization algorithms, left unconstrained, search the parameter space to *maximize* those noisy metrics.

This combination—noisy inputs, noisy objectives, and powerful optimizers—is a recipe for overfitting. The more flexible the model (more parameters, more degrees of freedom in weights), the more room the optimizer has to align itself with random quirks of the sample.

Regularization and constraints are your main defenses. They:

- Limit the complexity and extremity of the solutions.
- Encode prior beliefs about stability, diversification, and cost.
- Reduce variance of parameters and portfolios across samples, even at the price of some bias.

The art of quantitative investing is not to find the optimizer that squeezes the most Sharpe out of the backtest, but to design optimization problems—objectives, constraints, and regularization—that produce portfolios and models which *survive* the transition from backtest to live trading.

In subsequent chapters, we will revisit these ideas in more detail, examining how overfitting manifests in specific modeling frameworks and how to choose regularization schemes and validation protocols that keep the optimization machinery working for you, rather than against you.

Chapter 2

Data Integrity and Leakage

Most quants obsess over model architecture and ignore the quiet villain upstream: dirty, leaking data. This chapter shows how tiny violations of time, survivorship, and universe rules can manufacture spectacular but fake performance-and how to engineer point-in-time, research-grade datasets that your future self (and risk committee) can actually trust.

2.1 Point-in-Time Market Data Construction

In earlier chapters we treated the backtest as a sequence of decisions through time: at each date you observe some information, apply a rule or model, and trade. Up to now we have largely taken the data itself for granted. In practice, that assumption is where many otherwise competent research pipelines go wrong.

This section is about what it means for data to be *point-in-time* (PIT), and how to reconstruct—as faithfully as possible—the exact information set your strategy would have seen on each historical decision date.

We will see that this requires careful attention to identifiers, corporate actions, data revisions, and timestamps, not just prices and returns.

What "Point-in-Time" Really Means

Informally, data is point-in-time if, for every decision time t in your backtest, you only use information that a real trader could have known at that moment.

That sounds obvious, but it is surprisingly easy to violate. Many commercial data sets are deliberately cleaned, corrected, and adjusted so that they look tidy *today*. When you use these "latest and greatest" histories for backtesting, you are often letting your model benefit from corrections and revisions that arrived *after* the decision date.

It helps to be precise. Fix a decision time t (for example, the close of 31 December 2018). There are three distinct notions of time to keep in mind:

- **Event time:** when something actually happened in the real world, such as a company announcing earnings at 4:05pm.
- **Availability (or arrival) time:** when that event became visible in your data feed or database; sometimes this is later than the real-world event time due to processing or vendor lag.
- **Effective time:** the first time at which it is appropriate to *use* the event in your model. For example, an index reconstitution announced on one date but effective on a later date.

We say that a data set is *point-in-time correct* for decision time t if, when you run your backtest:

1. Every data item used for the decision at t has an availability time $\leq t$, and
2. Where applicable, the item's effective time is also $\leq t$.

You can think of your backtest as moving forward along a timeline. At each step t, you freeze the world and ask: "What did I know then?"

Point-in-time construction is simply the discipline of answering that question honestly, for every single bar.

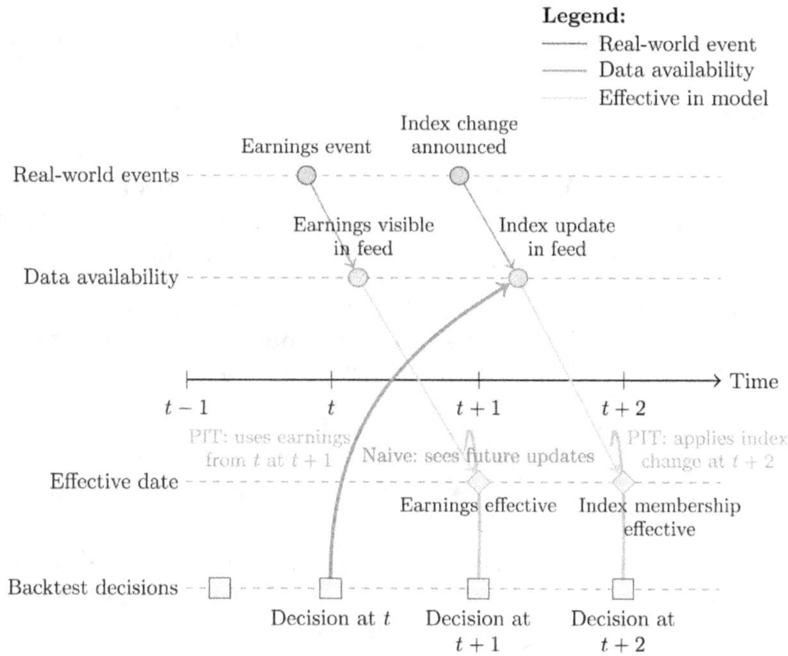

This may look like a technical subtlety, but it is one of the deepest practical issues in quantitative research. If you get point-in-time construction wrong, no amount of sophisticated modelling can rescue the validity of your backtest.

Naive Vendor Histories versus Point-in-Time Views

Most data vendors have two competing goals:

1. Provide a clean, corrected view of history for *analysis today*.
2. Provide a realistic historical view for *simulation as of past dates*.

These goals are in tension. For example:

- A stock's earnings per share for 2019 might be restated in 2021. For analytical users, it is nice if the vendor simply stores the latest, corrected EPS and applies it to the entire 2019 history.
- An index provider may rebalance membership every quarter, but your vendor might store a convenience file of "current constituents" that does not track historical changes.
- Corporate actions such as splits and special dividends are often reflected by adjusting the entire historical price series so that it is smooth and contiguous, without gaps or jumps.

All of these conveniences are helpful for descriptive analysis, factor correlations, or charting. They are *dangerous* in backtesting, because they silently alter what was knowable in the past.

A genuinely point-in-time backtest, in contrast, asks for a *time slice* of the database at each decision date. That time slice is constructed based on the arrival and effective times of each record, not just the calendar date to which it is logically attached.

Stable Keys and the Problem of Identifiers

Before we talk about prices, fundamentals, and revisions, we need to address a simpler but crucial piece: how you identify each security through time.

Many common identifiers are not stable:

- **Tickers** can change when companies rebrand, merge, or move exchanges.
- **Exchange codes** can change as firms cross-list or migrate.
- **ISINs or CUSIPs** can change during certain corporate events or reclassifications.

If you join tables on tickers alone, you risk aligning today's ticker with yesterday's data for a *different* company, or losing historical records when tickers are recycled. A typical symptom is a backtest that "drops" entire histories around corporate events, or that inexplicably creates or destroys alpha when you change your join keys.

The cure is to use a **permanent identifier**, such as a vendor-specific security ID, that is guaranteed not to change over the life of the instrument. The workflow is:

1. Build or obtain a *security master*: a table that links permanent IDs to time-varying attributes (tickers, names, exchanges) with validity date ranges.
2. When you ingest any data set (prices, fundamentals, corporate actions), map its identifiers to your permanent ID using the security master, respecting those date ranges.
3. In all subsequent joins and backtests, use the permanent ID as the key.

This is mundane engineering, but without it you cannot reliably reconstruct who was who at any given time, which undermines point-in-time reconstruction from the start.

Corporate Actions and Price Histories

Corporate actions—splits, cash dividends, stock dividends, spin-offs, rights issues—affect the price and share count of a security. To keep charts smooth and return calculations simple, vendors often provide *adjusted prices*:

- **Split-adjusted:** historical prices are scaled so that a 2-for-1 split appears as a continuous series instead of an overnight halving of price.
- **Dividend-adjusted:** historical prices are further adjusted to remove the downward jump on ex-dividend dates, making the total return path visually smoother.

For many applications, these convenient adjusted series are fine. But they can create subtle look-ahead issues in backtests:

- The adjustment factor for a split that occurs on date t is applied retroactively to all prior dates in the history. A naive backtest that uses the adjusted series at time $t-1$ is therefore benefiting from knowledge of a split that has not yet happened.
- Some vendors recompute adjustment factors when late corporate actions are processed or when past dividends are corrected. Again, using the "latest" adjusted history at every past date gives you a view that no real trader had at the time.

A point-in-time approach separates two layers:

1. **Raw facts**: unadjusted close prices, share counts, declared dividends with ex-dates, and split ratios, all stamped with their announcement, effective, and arrival times.
2. **Derived series**: for example, the split- and dividend-adjusted close that is appropriate to use for return computation at decision time t.

The key is that your adjustment calculations must be applied *only using events whose availability and effective times are* $\leq t$. Practically, this means that for each bar t you compute an adjustment factor based on the corporate actions known up to that point, and apply it forward or backward *only as justified* by your modelling assumptions.

A pragmatic compromise that many practitioners use is:

- Store raw prices and a full corporate actions history.

- For each backtest run, construct an adjusted price series on the fly, but enforce a rule such as "do not let the price at t be altered by an action that becomes public after the close of t." This might mean that the same calendar date has different numerically adjusted prices depending on when you run the backtest, which is uncomfortable but honest.

The main message is that you should treat vendor-adjusted histories as *derived convenience views*, not as ground truth; for point-in-time work, you want to be in control of the adjustment logic.

Revisions and Late-Arriving Information

Fundamental data and classifications introduce another dimension: revisions. A company may:

- Release an earnings statement, then file an amended version later.
- Restate several years of financials due to an accounting change.
- Be reclassified from one sector or industry to another.

If your database simply stores the "current best" version of each fundamental field, your backtest may accidentally use information that was not available at the time. For example, when you screen in 2015 for low price-to-book stocks, your query might be using book values that include restatements made in 2017.

To handle this properly, each record must carry at least two dates:

- **As-of date:** the period or reporting date the data describes (e.g., fiscal year-end 2014-12-31).
- **Availability date:** when this specific value became available in your database (e.g., the date the filing was processed by the vendor).

If there are revisions, you will have multiple records with the same as-of date but different availability dates. A point-in-time query at decision time t should select the latest record whose availability date is $\leq t$.

The same idea applies to:

- **Index membership:** track not only the date a stock is added or removed, but when that change was announced and when your system learned about it.
- **Ratings and classifications:** credit ratings, analyst recommendations, sector codes all have change dates and possible backfills.

A convenient mental model is to think of your database as a sequence of "snapshots" over time. At each snapshot date t, the database contains the best information available up to that point. Revisions add new layers on top of old ones, but they do not retroactively edit the past for backtesting purposes.

Building a Point-in-Time Data Pipeline

Putting these pieces together, how do you actually implement point-in-time construction in a research environment?

1. Ingest Raw Vendor Feeds with Rich Timestamps

When you load data from vendors, resist the temptation to flatten or simplify. Instead:

- Preserve all relevant dates: event date, announcement date, effective date, and the date you imported the record.
- Map all securities to a permanent ID using your security master.
- Keep separate tables for raw prices, corporate actions, fundamentals, and classifications, rather than prematurely merging them.

The goal is to maintain enough detail that you *could* reconstruct a snapshot of the database as it looked on any past day.

2. Store Revisions Rather Than Overwriting

Design your storage so that new information adds rows instead of overwriting old values. For example, a simple scheme for fundamentals might be:

- One row per (security, as-of date, version), with an availability timestamp.
- A point-in-time query chooses the row with the largest availability timestamp up to the decision time.

This is sometimes called a "slowly changing dimension" approach in data warehousing. It adds storage cost but is cheap insurance against subtle look-ahead.

3. Materialize Time-Slices for Backtests

When you run a backtest, you need an efficient way to ask: "What did I know at each decision date along this path?" There are two common architectures:

- **On-the-fly queries:** At each time step t, query your underlying tables with conditions like availability_time $\leq t$, and compute the derived features. This is flexible but can be slow if your universe and feature set are large.
- **Precomputed snapshots:** Ahead of time, build a "PIT feature store" that contains, for each (security, decision date), the features and labels you would have had access to at that date. Backtests then read from this store like they would from a static panel.

The second option pays a higher upfront cost but makes experimentation much faster, and it centralizes the tricky temporal logic in one place where it can be audited and tested.

4. Align Decision Times with Data Availability

Finally, you must be clear about the clock you are using for decisions. For example:

- If you trade on the open using yesterday's close and any news or fundamentals published before the open, your decision time is just before the open, and your availability cutoff should be that same time.

- If you trade at the close using intraday signals, your decision time is just before the close, and you should not use data that only solidifies in the post-close window.

In backtests, a common simplification is to treat days as atomic units and to assume that anything with an availability date of t is usable for a trade executed at the *next* bar (e.g., use information from day t to trade at day $t+1$). This prevents you from accidentally using truly same-day post-close information to trade on that same close.

The crucial step is to encode these assumptions explicitly in your time-slicing logic, and to apply them consistently across all features and assets.

Why This Level of Rigor Matters

From a distance, point-in-time construction looks like a lot of plumbing. It is tempting to view it as an engineering detail and to focus on models and signals instead. That is backwards.

The entire premise of a backtest is that it tells you something about how a strategy would have behaved in the past under realistic conditions. If your data stack allows even small amounts of future information to leak into the past, you are no longer simulating history; you are grading your model on an exam for which it has already seen the answers.

A robust, point-in-time data pipeline:

- Forces you to be explicit about what information is available when.
- Protects you from many subtle forms of leakage that are hard to detect later.
- Provides a solid base on which to implement the more advanced bias controls and leakage audits we will develop in subsequent sections.

In short, without point-in-time market data construction, all subsequent model evaluation is suspect, no matter how impressive the machine learning or optimization layers that sit on top.

2.2 Corporate Actions, Revisions, and Alignment Pitfalls

In the previous section, we focused on building a point-in-time (PIT) view of the world: at each decision date, the backtest should only see information that was truly available then. We discussed identifiers, timestamps, and the idea of reconstructing a historical "snapshot" of the database.

In this section, we take that framework and apply it to three particularly treacherous areas:

- How we handle *corporate actions* such as dividends and splits.
- How we deal with *revisions and restatements* to fundamentals and classifications.
- How we *align** prices, returns, and fundamentals on the calendar.

In all three cases, tiny implementation details can cause your backtest to quietly use future information, or to measure returns in a systematically distorted way. The end result is the same: you think you have found a robust edge, when in reality you have found a data artifact.

Corporate Actions: Why Adjustments Matter

Corporate actions change either the number of shares outstanding, the price per share, or both. Common examples include:

- **Stock splits and reverse splits** (e.g., 2-for-1, 1-for-10).
- **Cash dividends** and **stock dividends**.

- **Spin-offs**, rights issues, and bonus issues.

If you simply look at raw closing prices, these events produce jumps that are not economic returns:

- In a 2-for-1 split, the price roughly halves, but shareholders now own twice as many shares. Wealth is unchanged.
- On the ex-dividend date, the price drops by approximately the dividend amount, but shareholders receive the dividend in cash. Again, wealth is (approximately) unchanged.

If you naively compute returns as today's price divided by yesterday's price minus one, these mechanical jumps show up as huge negative (or positive) returns. Strategies that try to exploit those "moves" are chasing accounting events, not real opportunities.

To avoid this, vendors often provide *adjusted prices*:

- **Split-adjusted prices** rescale the historical series so that splits vanish and the time series is smooth.
- **Dividend-adjusted prices** further adjust for cash payouts, so that the adjusted series tracks the *total return* of holding the stock (price plus dividends reinvested).

For descriptive analysis, charts, and simple return calculations, these adjusted series are extremely convenient. But from a point-in-time perspective, they come with a catch: many adjustment schemes apply the full effect of an event to *all prior history*, using knowledge of corporate actions that have not yet occurred at earlier dates.

Retroactive Adjustments as Look-Ahead

Consider a split that happens on date T. A typical vendor will compute an adjustment factor and multiply *every* price before T by that factor so the time series is smooth. From the perspective of someone looking at the data today, this is great: you do not see any discontinuities.

From the perspective of a trader living on date $T - 30$, this is impossible. The prices they saw at the time were not yet adjusted for a split that lay 30 days in the future. If your backtest uses the fully adjusted historical series as if it had always looked that way, you have allowed future information—knowledge of the split and its details—to flow back in time.

The same logic applies to accumulated dividend adjustments. If the vendor recomputes the adjustment factors when new dividends are announced or corrected, the entire past trajectory is updated. Unless you recreate the adjustment state as of each date, you are effectively giving your model the benefit of hindsight about the pattern of future dividends.

This is a classic form of look-ahead bias that rarely shows up as an obvious error. Your code might be perfectly written; the issue lies in the assumptions baked into your data source.

Robust Corporate Action Handling

The goal is not to reject adjusted prices altogether, but to control *how* adjustments enter your backtest so they do not reveal the future. A practical, robust approach has three layers:

1. Store Corporate Actions Explicitly

First, ingest corporate actions into dedicated tables, separate from prices:

- For splits: ratio, announcement date, effective date, and the time you learned about it.
- For dividends: amount, currency, ex-date, record date, payment date, and availability date.
- For spin-offs and similar events: details of the distribution and the mapping between parent and child securities.

Each record should be linked to the security via a permanent identifier, as discussed in the previous section, and stamped with the relevant timestamps (event, effective, and availability times).

2. Keep Raw Prices as Ground Truth

Second, store and preserve *raw* price data: the unadjusted closes, opens, highs, lows, and volumes. These are the prices that actually traded, and they define your execution environment. Treat these as your canonical time series.

Adjusted prices can be derived on top of these raw series, but raw data should remain intact and queryable. If you overwrite raw prices with adjusted values, you lose the ability to reason cleanly about what happened when.

3. Compute Adjusted Series Point-in-Time

Third, when you do need adjusted prices (for example, to compute returns that are comparable across events), compute them in a point-in-time fashion:

- For each decision date t, determine which corporate actions are *effective and known* by that date.
- Construct a cumulative adjustment factor based only on that subset of events.
- Apply the factor to the raw series for dates where you deem it appropriate (typically backward from the first affected date, but not into the future).

This means the adjusted price for a given calendar day may depend on the decision date from which you are viewing it. That feels strange at first, but it simply reflects the fact that your knowledge of the future changes as you move forward in time.

In practice, many teams compromise by defining a market convention, such as:

> Use prices that are adjusted for all corporate actions with effective dates up to and including t, but ignore events with effective dates after t.

If the vendor's adjustment factors adhere to this convention (and are documented clearly), you can safely use the vendor's adjusted series. If not, you should build your own adjustment logic on top of raw data and explicit corporate action tables.

Revisions and Restatements: The Moving Target of Fundamentals

Corporate actions are not the only source of time inconsistency. Fundamental data and classifications are frequently revised:

- A company releases preliminary earnings, then files a final version.
- Accounting changes cause several years of financial statements to be restated.
- Sector or industry classifications are updated, sometimes with backfilled history.

From the perspective of an analyst working today, it is natural to want the "most accurate" numbers. Vendors respond to that demand by updating their databases to reflect the best available information, often replacing old values with new ones.

From a backtesting perspective, we care about something different: what numbers did a trader *actually see* at the time they made their decisions? That includes all the messiness of preliminary estimates, reporting lags, and occasional errors.

As-Of Dates versus Availability Dates

To handle this properly, we must distinguish at least two dates for each fundamental observation:

- The **as-of date**: the period the data describes (e.g., fiscal year-end, quarter-end).
- The **availability date**: when the value became usable in your system (e.g., filing date plus processing lag).

Revisions enter the picture when we have multiple records with the same as-of date but different availability dates. A realistic, point-in-time view at decision date t should use the *latest* record whose availability date is $\leq t$.

For example, suppose:

- On March 15, a company reports preliminary earnings for the quarter ended February 28.
- On April 10, it files an amended statement correcting an error.
- On June 1, the vendor identifies a data entry mistake and corrects the database.

A decision on March 20 should use the preliminary number; a decision on April 20 can use the amended number; a decision on June 15 can use the corrected number. What you should not do is run a backtest for 2010–2020 and let every past date use the post-June 1 value as if it had always been known.

Classification Revisions

Industry, sector, and index classifications behave similarly. Global classification schemes are periodically updated; index providers reconstitute membership; sometimes vendors retroactively apply new classifications back in time.

If you build a strategy that depends on "current sector" or "current index membership" without tracking when those labels were introduced, you may inadvertently label past states using future knowledge. For example, a stock added to an index in 2020 might be backfilled as "index member" for earlier years in a naive file, even though no one in 2015 knew it would eventually join.

The same point-in-time discipline applies: treat classifications as time-varying attributes with change dates and availability dates, and ensure that your backtest only uses labels that were active and known at each decision time.

Calendar Alignment Pitfalls

Even if you handle corporate actions and revisions properly, you can still corrupt your backtest by misaligning time series. Misalignment errors are often small—one bar off here, one day off there—but their impact on performance metrics can be large.

Three types of alignment deserve special attention:

- Price and return alignment.
- Fundamentals and price alignment.
- Cross-market or cross-asset calendar alignment.

Price and Return Alignment

A surprisingly common bug is off-by-one misalignment between prices and returns. For example:

- You compute a signal based on closing prices on date t.
- You intend to trade at the close of t and measure the return from t to $t + 1$.
- But in your code, you accidentally align the signal with the return from $t - 1$ to t, or from t to $t + 1$ in a way that implicitly uses information from the very return you are trying to predict.

In time series, such off-by-one errors can make predictive relationships look stronger than they are. A model that should be predicting *next* period's return ends up "predicting" the same period's return, or a return that has already taken place.

Robust practice is to make the prediction and execution lags explicit in your data pipeline. For example, you might adopt the convention:

> Signals computed from data with date t are used to trade at the *next* bar, and returns from t to $t + 1$ are the outcome.

Then, in your feature construction, you systematically shift features and labels by one bar (or more, if your process requires longer lags) and test that there is no accidental overlap.

Fundamentals and Price Alignment

Aligning fundamentals to prices is even more delicate. A typical pattern is:

- A company has a fiscal quarter ending at date T.
- It reports the results with some delay (e.g., $T + 40$ days).
- You want to use those fundamentals in a strategy that trades daily.

A naive implementation might:

- Forward-fill the fundamental value from as-of date T across all calendar dates until the next report.
- Use that value together with daily prices to compute factors like earnings yield or return on equity.

If you forward-fill starting at T itself, you are implicitly assuming that the market knew the final numbers at T, which is false. The right choice is to start forward-filling *no earlier than the availability date,* and to only use the value in backtests from that date onward.

Every data vendor makes choices about how to "align" fundamentals with prices for convenience. Some provide multiple date fields (as-of, announcement, effective) and recommended practices. Others provide a pre-aligned panel without clearly stating the convention. As a practitioner, you should:

- Understand the vendor's alignment rules.

- Where necessary, rebuild your own alignment using raw dates.
- Enforce a minimum lag (e.g., use fundamentals with a 1-day or 2-day lag after the announcement) to model realistic processing delays.

Cross-Market and Cross-Asset Calendars

Strategies that span multiple assets or markets introduce another alignment challenge: not all exchanges and asset classes share the same calendar or time zone.

Common issues include:

- Joining two time series by date without accounting for holidays or half-days on one exchange but not the other.
- Combining daily equity returns (based on local close-to-close) with daily futures returns (based on a different cut-off) without adjusting for the time-of-day mismatch.
- Using global macro releases (which have specific timestamps) and aligning them to daily bars without considering whether they occurred before or after the market close in each region.

The result can be a strategy that appears to "anticipate" events that, in reality, happened after the trading decision time for some assets. To avoid this, you should:

- Standardize all timestamps to a reference time zone in your database.
- Track the trading hours and holidays for each asset and exchange.
- Define for each strategy a clear decision time (e.g., New York close) and only use information that is available before that time in each market.

Practical Alignment and Adjustment Guidelines

To make these ideas concrete, here is a set of practical guidelines you can apply in your own research stack:

- **Separate raw and derived data.** Keep raw prices, volumes, fundamentals, and corporate actions in their own tables. Derive adjusted prices, returns, and features in a controlled, documented layer on top.
- **Track all relevant dates.** For every record, store at least: the period it describes (as-of), the effective date (if applicable), and the availability date (when you could have known it).
- **Avoid overwriting history.** When new information or corrections arrive, add new rows rather than editing old ones. Use availability dates to reconstruct which version was visible when.
- **Make lags explicit.** In feature and label construction, explicitly shift signals so that they use only data that would have been available before the execution time. Test for off-by-one and alignment errors as part of your standard QA.
- **Understand vendor conventions.** Read the documentation for your data sources. Know how they handle corporate actions, restatements, and timings. Where conventions are unclear or unsuitable for backtesting, rebuild your own.
- **Implement alignment checks.** Develop simple diagnostic scripts that, for a given asset and date range, print out the prices, returns, fundamentals, and corporate actions together with their timestamps. Visually inspect a sample to confirm that your alignment logic matches your conceptual model.

Why These Details Are Not Optional

It is tempting to think of corporate action handling, revision tracking, and calendar alignment as secondary to the "real work" of modelling. In reality, they are the foundation upon which all backtest results rest.

A model trained on misaligned or future-contaminated data is almost guaranteed to look better in-sample than it will out-of-sample. The apparent skill is often just the model picking up on artifacts:

- Pricing jumps around splits that have been smoothed away in hindsight.
- "Predictive" relationships between fundamentals and returns that arise because restated data was used as if it had been known earlier.
- Cross-asset timing patterns that depend on using information as of the wrong side of the clock.

These forms of leakage are especially insidious because they do not always produce obviously impossible trades; they simply inflate Sharpe ratios and compress drawdowns enough to push you over a decision threshold.

By handling corporate actions, revisions, and alignment with the same rigor you apply to model design, you dramatically reduce the chances that what you are seeing is an illusion. In the next section, we will formalize this intuition by laying out a taxonomy of data biases and leakage modes, and by introducing a systematic framework for auditing your entire research pipeline for these subtle but dangerous errors.

2.3 Taxonomy of Data Biases and Leakage

The previous sections have built a foundation: we defined point-in-time (PIT) data, examined how corporate actions and revisions must be handled through time, and discussed how calendar misalignment can quietly contaminate a backtest. We now widen the lens.

Even with careful PIT construction, there remain multiple ways in which your data and methodology can smuggle information from the future into the past or otherwise distort the sample you test on. Collectively, these problems sit under the heading of *data biases and leakage*.

This section offers a structured taxonomy of the most important types:

- Look-ahead bias.
- Survivorship bias.
- Selection bias.
- Label leakage (a family of related problems).

For each category we will explain:

- How it arises in typical quant workflows.
- How it inflates apparent performance.
- What practical diagnostics you can use to detect it.

Before diving into details, it helps to see the "map" of the territory.

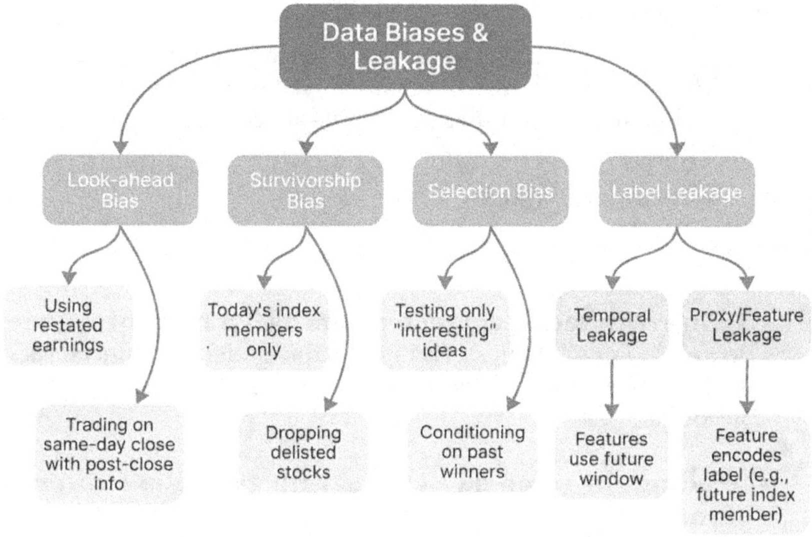

At the highest level, we can group these issues into two families:

- **Who is in the sample?** (survivorship and selection bias).
- **What information do features and labels contain, and when?** (look-ahead and label leakage).

We will examine each in turn.

Look-Ahead Bias

Look-ahead bias occurs when your backtest or model uses information that would not have been available at the time the trading decision is assumed to be made.

You can think of it as a violation of the basic rule introduced in the PIT section: at decision time t, you are only allowed to use data that is available and effective at or before t. Look-ahead bias breaks this rule, often in subtle ways.

How Look-Ahead Arises

Some common pathways:

- **Using restated or corrected data as if it had always been known.** For example, training a factor model on financial ratios where the denominators come from 2021 restatements of 2018 accounts.
- **Trading on same-day closes with post-close information.** For instance, using earnings announced at 4:05pm to trade at the 4:00pm close.
- **Using fully adjusted prices that embed future corporate actions.** As discussed earlier, vendor-adjusted series can effectively "know" about future splits or dividends when viewed from past dates.
- **Leaking target-period data into features or filters.** For example, filtering stocks based on realized volatility computed over a window that overlaps the returns you are trying to predict.

In all these cases, your backtest is answering the question: "Given what we know today about the past, how would this strategy have done?" That is not the same as: "Given what traders knew then, how would it have done?"

How It Inflates Performance

Look-ahead bias usually does two things:

- **Overstates predictability.** Your model is allowed to condition on variables that are tightly related to the outcome because they partly reflect it (or events closely following it).
- **Understates risk.** Since extreme events are often revised, corrected, or reclassified, using the final view of history can smooth drawdowns and volatility.

The net result is an overly optimistic Sharpe ratio and confidence in a signal that will fade or disappear in live trading.

Practical Diagnostics

Some simple checks:

- **Shift tests.** Intentionally shift your features back in time by one or more bars. If the performance drops dramatically when everything is lagged appropriately, the original setup probably contained look-ahead.
- **Timestamp audits.** For a few securities and dates, print out the raw records with their availability dates and verify that no field used in the strategy has an availability date after the decision date.
- **Sanity constraints.** Codify rules such as "never trade on the same bar as an earnings announcement" unless you explicitly model intraday timing, and test that the backtest respects them.

Survivorship Bias

Survivorship bias occurs when your sample includes only those assets that survived to the end of the sample period (or to the present), and excludes those that went bankrupt, were delisted, or otherwise disappeared.

How Survivorship Bias Arises

Common sources include:

- **Using today's index members for the whole history.** For example, backtesting a strategy on current S&P 500 constituents all the way back to 1990, implicitly assuming those firms were in the index throughout and ignoring those that dropped out.

- **Vendor coverage limited to active securities.** Some cheap or retail-oriented data sets only include firms that are currently listed or actively traded.
- **Dropping delisted stocks during cleaning.** If your data pipeline automatically removes securities with missing prices after a certain date, you may silently exclude underperformers that delisted.

In all these cases, you are analysing a world where the losers quietly vanish from the record.

How It Inflates Performance

Survivorship bias makes investment strategies look better than they truly are because:

- The worst-performing securities are more likely to delist or go bankrupt, so they are systematically removed.
- Portfolios constructed on the surviving universe will have higher average returns and lower volatility than portfolios that had to live through all the failures.
- Turnover and trading frictions associated with "bad outcomes" (e.g., forced liquidations at distressed prices) are understated.

The bias can be dramatic, especially for long horizons, small-cap universes, or strategies that explicitly target distressed names.

Practical Diagnostics

To detect survivorship bias:

- **Check coverage through time.** Plot the number of securities in your universe by year. An implausibly flat or upward-sloping count, with no drops during crisis years, is a red flag.
- **Inspect delisting codes.** Verify that you have price paths and delisting information for securities that disappear, and that they remain in the universe until the delisting date.

- **Compare against known historical index counts.** For major indices, the number of constituents and turnover are documented; your reconstructed universe should roughly match those patterns.

Rigorous universe construction, discussed later in the chapter, is essentially about eliminating survivorship bias by design.

Selection Bias

Selection bias concerns *how* you choose which strategies, assets, or time periods to analyse. Unlike survivorship, which is about who remains in the data set, selection bias is about how your own choices, guided by hindsight, tilt the playing field.

How Selection Bias Arises

Some typical patterns:

- **Testing only ideas that look promising ex post.** For example, after noticing that tech stocks have performed well recently, you design and test factors that overweight tech, ignoring all the ideas you did not pursue because they looked less appealing.
- **Conditioning on past winners.** You build a strategy only on assets or styles that have done well historically, excluding underperformers from consideration.
- **Cherry-picking sample periods.** You evaluate a mean-reversion strategy only over crisis periods where volatility was high, or a carry strategy only during low-rate regimes, because that is where they shine.
- **Researcher degrees of freedom.** You implicitly try many parameter combinations, universe definitions, and filters, but only report the best-performing configuration.

In all cases, the set of "experiments" you see in your notebook is not representative of all the experiments you effectively conducted in your head, or in code.

How It Inflates Performance

Selection bias is a cousin of overfitting:

- The more you search, the more likely you are to find something that looks good by chance, even if no true signal exists.
- By reporting only the winners, you systematically overstate the expected performance of a randomly chosen strategy from your research process.

Unlike look-ahead or survivorship, selection bias often does not show up as an obvious mistake in code. It lives in the research process itself.

Practical Diagnostics

While you cannot fully eliminate human judgment, you can:

- **Track the number of trials.** Keep a simple log of how many ideas, parameter sets, and universe definitions you tested. If the final "winner" was chosen from hundreds of candidates, its backtest Sharpe should be heavily discounted.
- **Use held-out validation periods.** Design your process so that model selection happens on one set of dates, and performance evaluation on another, untouched set.
- **Pre-register parts of your protocol.** For more serious research, commit ahead of time to which metrics, horizons, and evaluation rules you will use, to reduce the temptation to tailor them ex post.

Label Leakage

Label leakage is a broad family of problems in which your features contain information that is too closely related to the target you are trying to predict, typically by accident. In time-series language, you can think of label leakage as "the label leaking into the features."

It is especially common in machine learning workflows, where features are constructed automatically or in high dimension.

We can distinguish two overlapping subtypes:

- **Temporal leakage:** features reach into the future.
- **Proxy/feature leakage:** features are functions of, or proxies for, the label.

Temporal Leakage

Temporal leakage is closely related to look-ahead bias but worth highlighting separately because it often appears in feature engineering.

Examples include:

- **Using realized volatility windows that straddle the prediction horizon.** For instance, you define a feature as volatility over days t to $t + 20$, and then try to predict the return from t to $t+5$. The feature directly uses information from part of the future path you are predicting.
- **Using rolling averages that include the current bar to predict the current bar.** For example, using a 20-day moving average that includes price at time t to "predict" return from t to $t + 1$, but accidentally computing the return from $t - 1$ to t.
- **Normalizing by future quantities.** Such as scaling a feature by total volume over the coming week, then predicting next-day return.

These design choices often arise innocently: a convenient library function for rolling windows, an off-by-one in indices, or reuse of a feature from a different problem where it was appropriate.

Proxy / Feature Leakage

Proxy leakage occurs when a feature encodes the label in disguise, or contains post-event information that is highly correlated with the label.

Examples:

- **Using future index membership as a feature.** For example, marking stocks as "eventual index members" years before they are added, and trying to predict returns over that period. The feature identifies winners (according to the index provider) ahead of time.

- **Including labels or close derivatives thereof in the feature set.** A classic mistake is to include next-period return or a smoothed version of it as a feature by accident, due to sloppy column naming or index alignment.
- **Using post-trade quantities that depend on the realized return.** For example, "realized P&L over last week" as a feature for predicting next week's return, where the P&L was computed using the model itself.

In machine learning settings, leakage of this sort can result in spectacular in-sample performance and near-random out-of-sample performance, because the model has effectively memorized the answer key.

How Label Leakage Inflates Performance

Label leakage makes the prediction problem artificially easy:

- Correlations between features and labels are stronger than they would be in reality, because the features are informed by the labels.
- Model complexity can exploit these correlations to achieve very high training and even cross-validation scores if the data splitting is not strictly time-respecting.

A tell-tale sign is that simpler models (e.g., linear regression) perform almost as well as complex ones in-sample but both collapse out-of-sample; or that performance drops sharply when you tighten the time separation between feature and label.

Practical Diagnostics

To uncover label leakage:

- **Draw time diagrams.** For each major feature, sketch which time indices it uses and compare them to the prediction horizon. If any feature touches or overlaps the future relative to the label, it is suspect.
- **Check for duplicates and near-duplicates.** Verify that no feature column is just a shifted version of the label, and that no combination of features can trivially reconstruct the label.

- **Permutation tests.** Randomly permute labels across time or across securities. If performance remains surprisingly high, your model is probably using non-causal structure or leakage.

A Simple Leakage Audit Framework

Putting all of this together, it is useful to have a lightweight "leakage audit" you can run on any research pipeline. A practical checklist:

- **Information timing audit.** For a sample of features and dates, confirm that every input used at decision time t has an availability time $\leq t$, and that trading decisions use a consistent lag relative to market close or open.
- **Universe audit.** Verify that the investable universe at each date is defined using only information available at that time, includes delisted securities until their exit, and does not rely on future index membership or coverage files.
- **Feature construction audit.** For each feature, document which raw fields and time indices it uses. Look explicitly for windows that overlap the prediction horizon or use post-event labels.
- **Process audit.** Keep a simple record of how many ideas and parameter sets you have tried, and use held-out periods for honest evaluation of the final choice.

This discipline may feel heavy at first, but it quickly becomes routine. More importantly, it shifts your mindset: instead of asking only "How good is this backtest?", you also ask "How could this backtest be lying to me?"

In the final section of this chapter, we will apply these concepts to one of the most pervasive sources of bias in practice: how we define the investable universe and control for survivorship.

2.4 Universe Definition and Survivorship Control

By now we have established two key ideas. First, all data used in a backtest must be point-in-time: at each decision date you may only see what a real trader could have known then. Second, even if each individual data field is point-in-time, your overall research process can still suffer from structural biases such as look-ahead, selection bias, and survivorship bias.

This section focuses on one of the most pervasive and underappreciated sources of distortion: *how you define the investable universe.* The universe is the set of securities over which you compute signals, construct portfolios, and measure performance. Its definition embeds assumptions about:

- Which securities exist and when.
- Which securities are considered eligible for trading.
- How you treat entries (IPOs) and exits (delistings, bankruptcies, mergers).

If these assumptions are not made explicit and enforced in a point-in-time way, survivorship and selection biases quietly creep into every backtest, regardless of how careful you were with prices and fundamentals.

What Is an Investable Universe?

Conceptually, the investable universe at date t is the set of securities that meet your pre-specified eligibility rules at that date. These rules typically include:

- **Instrument type and exchange:** for example, common stocks listed on major exchanges, excluding preferred shares and OTC names.

- **Liquidity filters:** minimum average daily dollar volume, price thresholds, or spread constraints.
- **Corporate form filters:** excluding certain share classes, special purpose vehicles, or funds.
- **Index-based filters:** e.g., "only S&P 500 constituents."

The critical point is that this universe must be defined *point-in-time*. In other words, for each calendar date t you must ask:

> Given the rules we committed to, and given only information available up to t, which securities would we have considered tradable at t?

This sounds straightforward, but typical shortcuts break this discipline in subtle ways.

How Universes Embed Survivorship Bias

Survivorship bias arises when you only include securities that survive to the end of your sample (or to today), thereby omitting those that failed, delisted, or otherwise disappeared. Universe construction is the main conduit for this error.

Using Today's Index Members Back in Time

A very common practice is to take a current index membership list (say, today's S&P 500 constituents) and use those tickers for your entire backtest from, say, 1995 onward. The implicit assumption is:

> If a stock is in the S&P 500 today, we will treat it as if it was always relevant for our historical strategy.

This silently removes:

- Companies that were in the index in 1995 but later went bankrupt or were dropped.

- Firms that were small or illiquid for much of the history and only grew large enough to enter the index recently.

The resulting backtest lives in a kinder world where big losers never existed. That world is not the one your live strategy will face.

Coverage-Based Universes

Another variant is to construct your universe as "all securities present in my vendor's current coverage file." Many vendors only maintain ongoing data for currently listed companies; historical data for dead or delisted names may be incomplete, harder to access, or absent.

If you rely on such a coverage file without checking how it evolves through time, you effectively select a universe of survivors. The cleaner and more convenient the file looks, the more suspicious you should be.

Data Cleaning That Drops Losers

Even if your starting coverage is comprehensive, downstream cleaning steps can reintroduce survivorship bias. For example:

- Removing securities with "too many" missing prices, which naturally includes distressed firms that stopped trading often.
- Excluding securities that delisted for "bad" reasons (bankruptcy, non-compliance) because they behave differently or are "messy."

These decisions might be well-intentioned but, unless they are justified as part of a realistic implementability rule, they bias the universe toward winners.

Selection Bias through Universe Definition

Universe choices also introduce selection bias. Even if you include delisted securities, you may still condition your analysis on outcomes you can only see with hindsight.

Conditioning on Future Characteristics

Suppose you define your universe as "all stocks that at some point in the sample period had market cap above $10 billion" and then backtest from the start of the sample. You are selecting securities conditional on a future attribute (becoming large-cap). Early years of the backtest therefore include only those firms that will eventually succeed.

Similarly, defining a universe as "all stocks that at some point entered index X" conditions on future index membership. Strategies built on such a universe will look more robust than they truly are, because the sample is tilted toward stocks that passed a quality or size filter at some unknown future date.

Cherry-Picking Markets and Segments

Selection bias can also appear when you choose which markets or segments to include based on their apparent past performance. For example:

- Developing a value strategy only on markets that had strong value outperformance historically.
- Excluding countries or sectors that went through long bear markets, on the grounds that "they are different."

These choices are not always wrong, but you should recognise them as sources of selection bias. A carefully defined, point-in-time universe makes these decisions explicit and testable.

Principles of Robust, Point-in-Time Universe Construction

To avoid these pitfalls, universe construction should follow the same point-in-time discipline we applied to prices and fundamentals. The key principles are:

1. **Explicit rules.** Define your eligibility criteria in clear, implementable terms: exchange, instrument type, liquidity thresholds,

price filters, corporate form restrictions, and any index dependence.

2. **Time-varying membership.** For each date t, evaluate the rules using only information available at (or just before) t and record which securities pass.
3. **Complete life-cycle coverage.** Include securities from their first eligibility date until their true exit date (delisting, merger, etc.), with realistic exit prices.
4. **Separation of universe and signals.** Decide the universe independently from the signals you will later test, to reduce selection bias.

Let us unpack what this looks like in practice.

Implementing Point-in-Time Universes

1. Start from a Comprehensive Security Master

As with PIT data generally, you need a security master that:

- Assigns a stable, permanent identifier to each security.
- Records listing and delisting dates, exchange codes, instrument types, and share classes.
- Tracks corporate actions that create or retire securities (IPOs, mergers, spin-offs).

This master acts as the backbone: any universe definition starts from the set of all identifiable securities, not just those that happen to be trading today.

2. Encode Eligibility Rules

Next, specify and encode your eligibility rules in a way that your system can evaluate day by day. Typical elements include:

- **Exchange and instrument filters:** e.g., "primary listing on NYSE or NASDAQ; instrument type = common equity."
- **Liquidity filters:** e.g., "60-day average daily dollar volume above $1 million" and "price above $2."
- **Corporate form:** exclude ADRs, closed-end funds, or special share classes if they are not meaningfully tradable for your mandate.
- **Index or region filters:** if you restrict to certain indices or regions, use point-in-time membership based on historical constituent files.

For liquidity filters, remember that volume and price themselves are time-varying data. You must compute rolling averages using only past observations (no future bars in the window), and use a suitable lag so that the filter at date t uses data up to, say, $t - 1$.

3. Treat IPOs and New Listings Carefully

New securities should not appear in your universe before they are actually tradeable. For each security, determine:

- The first trading date that meets your data and liquidity requirements.
- Any seasoning period you require (e.g., "at least 20 trading days of history before eligibility").

Your universe file should then mark the security as "in universe" starting from the first date that both conditions are satisfied. Before that, the security simply does not exist as a candidate, even if you know today that it will eventually be important.

4. Handle Delistings and Exits Realistically

The other end of the life cycle is trickier and more consequential. For each security, you need:

- Its last trading date.
- The nature of its exit (merger, acquisition, bankruptcy, going private, etc.).
- The terminal value realised by a buy-and-hold investor (cash-out price, final trade, or zero in case of full default without recovery).

Your universe and backtest should:

- Keep the security in the universe until the delisting date (or until it fails your eligibility filters).
- Force any positions to be liquidated at a realistic price on or before the exit date, depending on the event's details.

Dropping securities from the universe earlier, or treating delistings as if they never occurred, both create survivorship bias. For distressed exits, in particular, you should resist the temptation to fill missing terminal prices with benign assumptions; those are precisely the bad outcomes your strategy must survive.

5. Build and Store a Universe File

Practically, many teams maintain a *universe file* with one row per (date, security) indicating whether the security is eligible for trading on that date. This file is constructed once, using the rules and data described above, and then used across all backtests.

Advantages include:

- **Consistency:** all strategies are evaluated on the same opportunity set.
- **Auditability:** you can inspect the universe on any date and understand which names were in or out and why.
- **Efficiency:** feature and signal computation can be restricted to the eligible universe, saving resources.

From a point-in-time perspective, the universe file is just another derived panel: at each date t it encodes what your trading system would have considered tradeable then.

Integrating Universe Definition with Backtests

Once you have a point-in-time universe, it must be integrated into every stage of the research pipeline:

- **Feature construction:** compute features only for securities in the universe on each date, or at least ensure that any downstream use respects universe membership.
- **Portfolio formation:** ensure that position sizing and optimisation only allocate to in-universe securities.
- **Performance measurement:** when computing averages, cross-sectional statistics, or factor portfolios, use the universe weights or membership flags, not the full coverage universe.

It is important that your universe definition be independent of the models you are testing. If the universe itself is tailored ex post to where a particular strategy performs well, you reintroduce selection bias at a higher level.

Why Survivorship Control Changes the Results

Survivorship and selection biases in the universe can dramatically inflate the apparent performance of a strategy. Controlling for them rarely makes your backtests look slightly worse; it often changes the conclusion from "compelling" to "marginal."

To see this, imagine two parallel backtests of the same simple strategy:

- One run on a survivorship-biased universe (e.g., today's index members backfilled).
- One run on a fully point-in-time, survivorship-controlled universe built as described above.

The first will typically show:

- Higher long-run compounded returns.
- Lower drawdowns, because catastrophic failures are missing.
- Slightly smoother behaviour in crisis periods, as weak names that experienced severe stress may have vanished from the sample.

The second will be more volatile, with lower average returns and uglier drawdowns-but it will be honest.

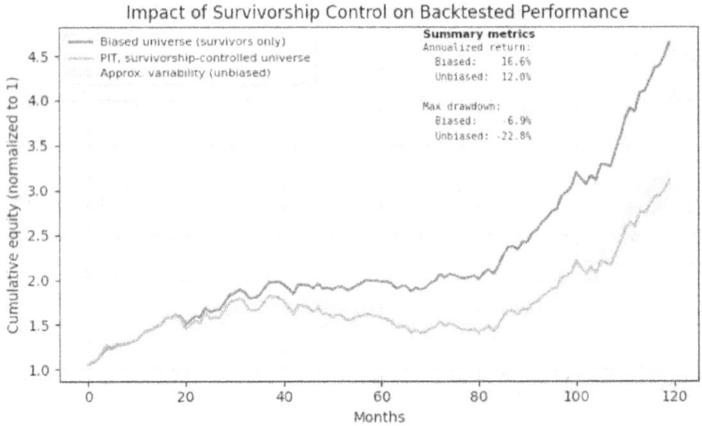

Figure 2.1: Illustrative equity curves for the same strategy tested on a survivorship-biased universe versus a point-in-time, survivorship-controlled universe. The biased universe shows higher returns and milder drawdowns, overstating the strategy's true robustness.

In real research, you should routinely perform such paired comparisons: run your strategy once on a naive universe (for diagnosis only) and once on your carefully constructed PIT universe. The gap between the two is an estimate of how much optimism survivorship and selection biases were adding.

Integrating Universe Construction into the Research Workflow

Finally, universe construction should not be an afterthought or a one-off script. It should be an integral, shared component of your research infrastructure:

- **Centralised definition:** maintain a small number of well-documented universes (e.g., "US large-cap," "Developed ex-US mid-cap") with explicit rules, rather than letting each researcher roll their own.
- **Version control:** treat universe definitions as code and data that can evolve, but must be versioned. If you change the liquidity threshold or exchange list, you should know which backtests used which version.
- **Automated checks:** run periodic diagnostics: number of names by date, entry and exit counts, distribution of delisting reasons, and comparison against external benchmarks (like official index membership histories).
- **Education and culture:** make it clear in your team that a strategy is not considered seriously tested until it has passed through the full point-in-time universe machinery.

When done well, robust universe definition fades into the background: it becomes a reliable part of your environment, much like a compiler or a database. When neglected, it becomes an invisible source of false confidence.

Viewed through the lens of this chapter, universe construction is not merely about "which stocks to include." It is about respecting the fundamental uncertainty of markets: in real time, you do not know which firms will survive, which will become blue chips, or which will quietly disappear. A point-in-time, survivorship-controlled universe forces your backtests to live in that same uncertain world.

Chapter 3

Validation and Robust Backtesting

Most backtests look impressive right up until you trade them. This chapter shows why: hidden look-ahead, sloppy cross-validation, and undisciplined hyperparameter searches quietly convert noise into "alpha." We rebuild the process from the ground up-starting with time-aware data splits and ending with capital-realistic simulations-so that every performance number in your research notebook has a clear, defensible chain of custody back to tradable reality.

3.1 Time-Aware Data Splitting Protocols

In earlier sections we treated overfitting mainly as a problem of model complexity and noisy signals. In finance, however, there is an additional, less visible enemy: time. Markets evolve, information arrives with lags, and trading decisions must be based only on what was known *then*, not what we know *now*.

Most machine-learning workflows assume data points are independent and identically distributed. A classical random train/test split shuffles observations and assigns, say, 70% to training and 30% to testing. This is acceptable for many cross-sectional problems (classifying images, predicting loan defaults), but it is fundamentally misaligned with financial time series, where order matters and dependence across time is strong.

This section explains how to slice data in a way that respects temporal ordering and information flow. We will:

- Contrast naive random splits with time-aware splits.
- Introduce chronological, rolling, and expanding windows.
- Explain purged and embargoed splits that handle overlapping events and subtle leakage.
- Provide practical guidelines and checklists so your whole pipeline obeys a strict "no future in the past" rule.

Why Random Splits Fail for Time Series

When you randomly shuffle daily returns or bar-level features and then split into train and test sets, you implicitly claim that:

- The joint distribution of features and labels does not change over time (stationarity).
- An observation on day t is effectively independent of an observation on day $t + 1$.

Neither assumption is remotely true in market data. Prices and derived features exhibit:

- **Serial dependence.** Today's return, volatility, order flow, and spreads are related to recent history.
- **Regime shifts.** The distribution in 2003 is not the same as in 2008, 2013, or 2020. Monetary policy, market structure, and participants change over time.
- **Non-stationarity.** Drifts, correlations, and risk premia evolve; features that work in one decade may die in the next.

Randomly mixing early and late periods therefore does two damaging things:

- It *breaks* the true temporal structure, making the learning problem artificially easier. A model can "see" future regimes while being trained, and then is conveniently tested on data from those same regimes.
- It *allows leakage.* Features or labels from the future can slip into the training set for predictions about the past, violating causality. For example, daily realized volatility computed using returns from t to $t+1$ might be used as a feature to predict a label at t, even though the $t+1$ return was not known at the decision time.

The result is a pleasant but misleading story: your backtests look stable, Sharpe ratios are high, and performance seems robust across "random" splits. Unfortunately, this realism evaporates when you try to trade, because the validation protocol never resembled real-time usage.

Time-aware data splitting protocols fix this by aligning the structure of your training and testing sets with the direction of time and the way you would actually deploy the model.

Simple Chronological Holdout

The simplest time-respecting split is a chronological holdout. You sort observations by time, use the early part for training, and keep the later part as a test set.

For example:

- Training set: January 2005 – December 2016.
- Test set: January 2017 – December 2019.

Every prediction in the test period is made using a model that only saw data from *before* that period. This mimics the real-world scenario where you would fit your model up to some "go-live" date and then trade it in the subsequent years.

Chronological splits solve the grossest violation—training on the future—but they still have limitations:

- You only get one test period, which may be unrepresentative (e.g., an unusually calm or turbulent market).
- You cannot assess how the model would have performed if launched at different times.
- If your model needs frequent re-estimation in production, a single static train/test split does not mimic that dynamic.

To address these issues, we move from one-off holdouts to moving windows.

Rolling and Expanding Windows

A more realistic paradigm for financial models is that they are re-estimated periodically as new data arrives. Time-aware splitting can emulate this through two related schemes:

- **Rolling windows (fixed-length).** The training window has constant length and rolls forward through time.
- **Expanding windows (growing history).** The training window starts at some initial date and expands as new data arrives; you never discard past data.

Rolling windows

In a rolling window setup, you choose a training window length (for example, 3 years of daily data) and a test horizon (for example, the next 3 months). Then you slide both windows through time.

A typical pattern might be:

- Train on 2010–2012, test on Q1 2013.
- Train on 2010 Q2–2013 Q1, test on Q2 2013.
- Train on 2010 Q3–2013 Q2, test on Q3 2013.

- ...and so on.

Characteristics:

- The model always uses a fixed span of recent history, which can be tuned to match the "memory" you believe markets have for this strategy.
- Old data is gradually dropped; if the strategy decays or regimes change, the model focuses on the most relevant environment.
- You get multiple train/test pairs, providing a distribution of out-of-sample results over different market periods.

Rolling windows are particularly appealing for strategies where you expect old data to be less informative, such as high-frequency trading or rapidly adapting signals.

Expanding windows

In an expanding window, you fix an initial start date and grow the training sample over time:

- Train on 2010, test on 2011.
- Train on 2010–2011, test on 2012.
- Train on 2010–2012, test on 2013.
- ...and so on.

Here, the model always has access to all historical data accumulated so far. This mirrors the behavior of a researcher who never throws data away but periodically refits on the complete history.

Characteristics:

- Useful when you believe more data is always helpful (e.g., low-frequency signals with slow decay).
- The effective sample size grows over time, so parameter estimates may become more stable.

- The influence of early data never fully disappears; if market structure shifted dramatically, very old observations can still tug on the model.

Choosing between rolling and expanding

The choice between rolling and expanding windows is largely about your beliefs regarding non-stationarity:

- If you think older data is actively misleading—for example, pre-decimalization or pre-electronic trading eras—a rolling window that forgets the distant past may be more appropriate.
- If you think the underlying relationship is persistent but noisy, and that market changes are gradual, an expanding window can provide stronger statistical power.

In both cases, the key virtue is that training and test periods respect time: test periods always lie strictly after the corresponding training periods.

Purged and Embargoed Splits: Handling Overlaps and Leakage

So far, we have only enforced that test data comes after training data. In practice, there is a subtler form of leakage that arises from *overlapping events*.

Consider these common patterns in trading strategies:

- You compute labels as forward returns over a horizon of H days (e.g., 5-day or 20-day returns).
- You hold positions for multiple days, so trades overlap in time.
- Features and labels for different timestamps depend on overlapping underlying returns.

If you naively assign timestamps to train and test sets based on their label date, information from the test set can indirectly influence the training set, and vice versa, through these overlaps.

Example: forward return labels.

Suppose your label at date t is the return from t to $t + 5$. Then:

- The label at t depends on returns $r_{t+1}, \ldots, r_{t+5}$.
- The label at $t + 3$ depends on $r_{t+4}, \ldots, r_{t+8}$.

These two labels share returns r_{t+4} and r_{t+5}. If the observation at t is in the training set and the observation at $t + 3$ is in the test set, the training data has already "seen" part of the future path that affects the test label. Even though you did not directly train on the exact test label, you trained on overlapping information.

This is leakage. It makes your model look more powerful than it really is, because you are allowing it to learn from returns that, in a real deployment, would not yet be known when making the decision.

Purged splits

Purged splits address this by removing from the training data any observations whose label windows overlap with the test label windows.

In practice:

- Decide on an event horizon H (for example, 20 trading days).
- When you choose a test period (say, all events whose label date is in 2018), identify all training events whose label windows intersect with those test label windows.
- Remove ("purge") those overlapping training events from the training set, even if their label dates lie earlier than the test dates.

Conceptually, you are carving out a clean separation in terms of the underlying information, not just the label timestamp. Any observation that draws on future returns that are also used for test labels is excluded.

This reduces effective sample size, which can feel painful, but it produces a more honest estimate of how the strategy will perform when labels do not share future information.

Embargoed splits

An additional refinement is to place an *embargo* window around the test set. The idea is to reserve a buffer of time just before and just after the test period where you do not use data for training.

Why is this needed? In many settings, even if label windows do not mathematically overlap, subtle dependencies exist near regime boundaries. For instance:

- A macro event (e.g., a central bank announcement) has effects that span several days or weeks.
- Corporate events may influence both pre-announcement drift and post-announcement reactions.

If you train on data just before the test period and those observations are tightly coupled with the test labels, the model may effectively peek across the boundary.

An embargoed split does the following:

- For a test period spanning dates $[T_{start}, T_{end}]$, define an embargo length E (e.g., 10 trading days).
- Exclude from training any observations whose label dates fall in $[T_{start} - E,\ T_{end} + E]$.

In other words, you surround the test period with a "no-train zone" of length E. This guards against spillover of information and cross-sectional dependencies that are hard to model explicitly.

Embargoing can be combined with purging: first purge overlapping label windows, then embargo around the test block to add a safety margin.

Visualizing Time-Aware Splits

The different splitting schemes are easier to grasp with a concrete timeline. Figure contrasts naive random splits with chronological, rolling, expanding, and purged/embargoed splits along a single time axis. Training and test regions are color-coded, and red shading marks leakage zones present under naive protocols but removed by the time-aware ones.

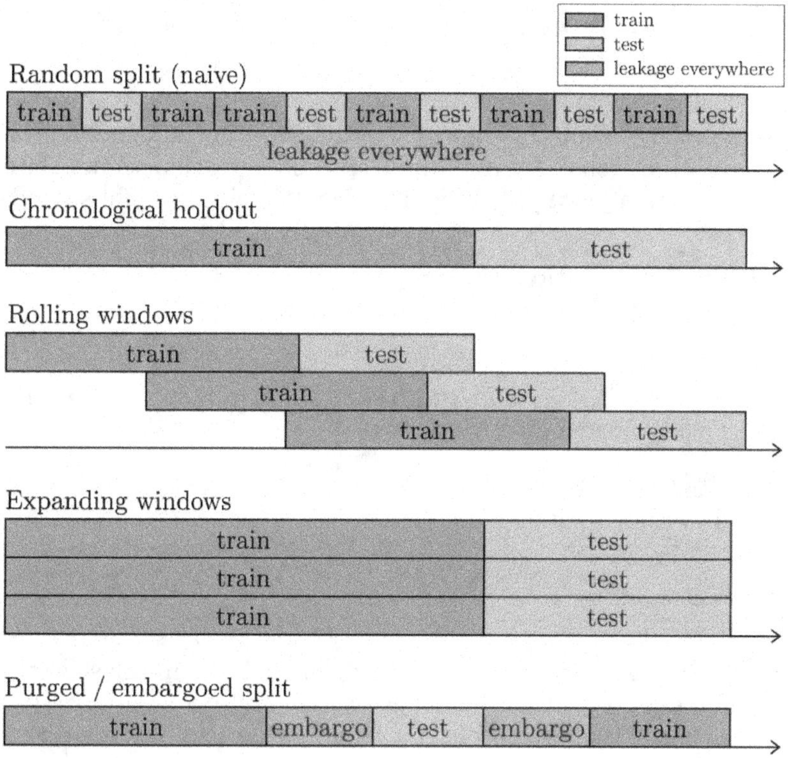

Practical Design Choices

Implementing time-aware data splits in a real research pipeline requires several concrete design decisions.

Split granularity

First, decide the natural time unit for splitting:

- **Bar-level** (e.g., 1-minute, 5-minute): suitable for intraday strategies; windows may be short but numerous.

- **Daily**: common for end-of-day strategies and factor models.
- **Monthly or quarterly**: better for low-frequency allocation or macro strategies.

The granularity should align with your rebalancing frequency and label horizon. If you rebalance monthly, a reasonable test block might be one or several months; if you trade intraday, test blocks might span days or weeks.

Window length and step size

Next, choose:

- The *training window length* (for rolling windows), or *initial history* (for expanding windows).
- The *test window length* and *step size* (how far you move the window each iteration).

Guidelines:

- Training windows should be long enough to capture several full cycles of your strategy's behavior (e.g., multiple volatility regimes or business cycles), but not so long that they include obsolete regimes.
- Test windows should be long enough to yield stable performance estimates but short enough to detect regime-dependent variation.
- The step size can be as small as one rebalancing period (maximal overlap of windows) or as large as the test window (non-overlapping evaluation periods).

Purging and embargo parameters

For purged/embargoed splits, you must set:

- **Event horizon H:** usually the maximum label horizon or holding period. Any two events whose label windows overlap within this horizon should not cross between train and test.
- **Embargo length E:** a buffer in time around each test period. A common heuristic is to set E equal to H or some fraction of it, depending on the persistence of the effects you study.

It is important to document these choices and to keep them fixed once your research protocol is defined; tuning H and E to improve backtest results is another form of overfitting.

Implementation Patterns and Checklists

To enforce a strict "no future in the past" principle across the entire pipeline, you should adopt both conceptual and technical safeguards.

Conceptual checklist

Before trusting any backtest, verify:

- **Time ordering:** Are all test observations strictly later than the training observations used to make predictions for them?
- **Label construction:** Do labels rely on future returns or events? If so, have you purged training observations whose label windows overlap with test label windows?
- **Data lags:** Are fundamentals, estimates, and alternative data aligned with their actual availability dates (not announcement dates alone)?
- **Rebalancing alignment:** Does the split granularity match the rebalancing frequency and decision horizon of the strategy?
- **Multiple evaluations:** If you perform many rolling or expanding window evaluations, are you summarizing performance as a distribution (rather than highlighting the single most favorable period)?

Pipeline patterns

On the technical side, structure your code so that it becomes difficult to violate temporal constraints inadvertently. For example:

- Centralize the logic that defines train/test indices based on time windows and reuse it across all models for a given project.
- Express windows in terms of date ranges (e.g., dictionaries mapping window ID to {train_start, train_end, test_start, test_end}) and pass these to your feature and label builders.
- At the point of feature construction, enforce that only data with timestamps $\leq$ decision time is accessible.
- If you are working with event-driven labels (e.g., earnings announcements), represent each event explicitly with start and end times, and use these to drive purging and embargoing.

Balancing Sample Size and Temporal Distance

A recurring trade-off in time-aware splitting is between:

- **More data, less realism:** Larger training samples and aggregated test periods reduce statistical noise but may blend across regimes and hide non-stationarity.
- **Less data, more realism:** Shorter, local windows better capture current dynamics and produce more honest assessments of how the strategy will fare soon after deployment, but at the cost of higher variance in estimates.

There is no universal optimum; the right balance depends on:

- The frequency and turnover of the strategy.
- The perceived stability of the underlying edge.
- The economic story behind the signal (slow-moving risk premia versus short-lived microstructure frictions).

In practice, it is wise to explore several reasonable window configurations and examine how performance varies. If the strategy's attractiveness hinges on a very specific window choice, that fragility is itself a cautionary signal.

From Splits to Credible Validation

Time-aware data splitting protocols are the foundation on which all other validation tools—time-series cross-validation, resampling, multiple testing control, and full backtest design—must rest. If you get the splits wrong, everything built on top of them is contaminated.

By moving from random splits to chronological, rolling, expanding, and purged/embargoed schemes, you align your research process with the way a trading model is actually used: learning from the past to make decisions about the future, under realistic information constraints. This alignment does not guarantee that your models will survive contact with the market, but it greatly increases the odds that failure in production reflects a genuine lack of edge, not a validation illusion created by temporal leakage.

3.2 Time-Series Cross-Validation and Resampling

In the previous section we imposed a basic discipline on our data splits: never let the model see the future when it is supposed to be predicting the past. That "no future in the past" rule is the minimum requirement for any credible backtest.

However, a simple chronological train/test split still leaves you with a coarse, often misleading view of model quality. You get one training period and one test period. If the test period happens to be unusually favorable (for example, a long bull market), you will overestimate how the model will age in production. If it is unusually hostile, you may prematurely discard a genuinely useful idea.

In classical machine learning, cross-validation solves this by slicing the sample into multiple folds, training and testing on different subsets, and aggregating the results. But standard k-fold cross-validation assumes that observations can be shuffled without breaking anything. For financial time series, shuffling destroys the very temporal structure we are trying to respect.

This section shows how to adapt cross-validation and resampling to dependent, non-stationary financial data. The goal is not just to get "a better accuracy number"; it is to build a realistic picture of how performance, risk, and parameter stability vary across time and regimes.

Why Standard k-Fold Cross-Validation Breaks in Time

In textbook k-fold cross-validation, you randomize the order of observations, split them into k equally sized folds, and then repeat:

1. Hold out one fold as test.
2. Train the model on the remaining $k - 1$ folds.
3. Evaluate on the test fold.
4. Cycle through all k choices of test fold.

This works under two strong assumptions:

- Observations are exchangeable: you can reorder them freely without changing the joint distribution.
- Dependencies, if any, are weak enough that shuffling does not fundamentally alter the learning problem.

For time series, neither assumption holds:

- **Temporal dependence.** Returns today are correlated with returns yesterday; volatility clusters; order flow is persistent.
- **Non-stationarity.** The distribution of returns, spreads, and volumes can change across years, months, or even days.

If you randomly shuffle and fold such data, you will inevitably place future observations into the training set for predictions about the past. The model is then evaluated as if it had access to future regimes, volatility states, and structural breaks that it could never have observed in reality.

The effect is a subtle but systematic optimism: the cross-validation scores look smoother and more favorable than they deserve. To fix this, we must re-think cross-validation so that each fold respects the direction of time.

Blocked and Rolling Time-Series Cross-Validation

Time-series cross-validation keeps the essential idea of multiple train/test splits but constrains the splits to be contiguous and time-ordered. There are two basic patterns:

- Blocked (or "forward chaining") cross-validation.
- Rolling-window cross-validation.

Both work on top of the time-aware data splits introduced earlier; they just apply them repeatedly to generate multiple, structured out-of-sample evaluations.

Blocked (forward-chaining) cross-validation

In blocked time-series cross-validation, you partition the timeline into k contiguous blocks and then, for each block in turn, use all *earlier* blocks for training and the current block as test.

For example, suppose you have daily data from January 2010 through December 2019 and you decide on five annual blocks:

- Block 1: 2010–2011
- Block 2: 2012–2013
- Block 3: 2014–2015

- Block 4: 2016–2017
- Block 5: 2018–2019

You might define the folds as:

Fold 1:	Train on Block 1, test on Block 2
Fold 2:	Train on Blocks 1–2, test on Block 3
Fold 3:	Train on Blocks 1–3, test on Block 4
Fold 4:	Train on Blocks 1–4, test on Block 5

Key features:

- Time ordering is respected: the model never trains on data later than the test block.
- Training sets grow as you move forward, reflecting how a live researcher accumulates history.
- Each fold tells you: "If I had started trading at the beginning of this test block, after training on everything before it, how would I have done?"

This is especially useful for low-frequency strategies where each block may span months or years. You get a sequence of realistic "launch dates" and can see how the strategy would have fared if launched at different points in history.

Rolling-window cross-validation

Rolling-window cross-validation is similar but fixes the length of the training window. Instead of always using all past data, you use only the most recent history of a specified length.

For instance:

- Training window: last 3 years of data.
- Test window: next 6 months.

Using our 2010–2019 example, a few folds might be:

- Fold 1: Train on 2010–2012, test on first half of 2013.
- Fold 2: Train on mid-2010–mid-2013, test on second half of 2013.
- Fold 3: Train on 2011–2013, test on first half of 2014.
- ...and so on.

Here:

- The training window length encodes your belief about how far back relevant information extends.
- By sliding the window, you repeatedly simulate "train on recent past, test on near future," which mimics periodic re-estimation in production.
- Because training windows overlap, each observation can participate in several folds, sometimes in training, sometimes in testing.

Rolling-window T-CV is particularly natural for higher-frequency strategies or for environments where you believe older data quickly becomes irrelevant or harmful.

Fold width and step size

To fully specify a time-series cross-validation scheme, you must choose:

- **Fold (test-block) width:** How long is each test period?
- **Step size:** By how much do you move the test window each time?

Guidelines:

- The test-block width should be at least several times your holding period, so that each fold includes many independent or weakly dependent trades. For example, if your strategy typically holds positions for 10 days, a 3-month test block is more informative than a 2-week block.
- The step size can be equal to the test-block width (non-overlapping folds) or smaller (overlapping folds). Smaller step sizes provide a finer-grained view of performance over time but increase computational cost and correlation between folds.
- For low-frequency strategies (monthly or quarterly rebalancing), yearly blocks and yearly steps are common. For intraday or daily strategies, you may use weeks or months.

The essential point is that folds are defined by contiguous time segments and that the training data for any fold always lies strictly before its test segment.

Interpreting Time-Series Cross-Validation Results

When you apply blocked or rolling T-CV, you no longer get a single performance number; you get a set of numbers, one per fold:

- Fold 1: Sharpe 1.2
- Fold 2: Sharpe 0.3
- Fold 3: Sharpe 0.9
- Fold 4: Sharpe -0.1

It is tempting to average these and report "mean Sharpe = 0.6, so the strategy works." That is already better than using a single test period, but it still throws away valuable information.

Instead, treat the collection of fold-level metrics as a rough empirical distribution of how the strategy behaves when launched at different times. Ask:

- How often is performance positive versus negative?
- How wide is the spread between good and bad periods?
- Do drawdowns cluster in certain regimes (e.g., crises, low-volatility environments)?
- Is there a trend: are recent folds weaker than older ones, suggesting decay?

This perspective supports several practical decisions:

- **Go/no-go decision.** If the strategy loses money in many folds or only looks attractive because of one very strong period, its edge is probably fragile or illusory.
- **Capital allocation.** Even if the average performance is acceptable, a wide dispersion suggests that you should size more conservatively or combine the strategy with others to smooth its behavior.
- **Monitoring in production.** The worst historical fold gives you a sense of how bad things can get. If live performance suddenly resembles the worst fold, that may trigger a review or de-risking.

Time-series cross-validation thus shifts your mindset from "What is the performance?" to "What is the distribution of possible futures for this strategy?"

Resampling Under Dependence: Block Bootstraps

Cross-validation provides variability across time, but it treats the observed sample as fixed. To quantify statistical uncertainty conditional on the observed time series structure, many researchers turn to bootstrapping—resampling the data with replacement to create pseudo-samples and computing the distribution of performance across those samples.

The naive bootstrap, which samples individual observations independently, breaks time dependence in the same way that random k-fold cross-validation does. For time series, you need resampling methods that preserve serial correlation. The standard tools are various forms of *block bootstrap*.

Basic block bootstrap

In the basic block bootstrap, you cut the time series into contiguous blocks of length L and resample these blocks with replacement to build new pseudo-series.

For a series of length T:

1. Construct overlapping or non-overlapping blocks:
    - Block 1: observations 1 to L.
    - Block 2: observations 2 to $L + 1$.
    - ...
    - Block $T - L + 1$: observations $T - L + 1$ to T.
2. Draw blocks at random with replacement until you accumulate at least T observations.
3. Stitch these blocks together in the order drawn to form a bootstrap series.

Because you resample blocks rather than individual points, local serial dependence (within each block) is largely preserved. By choosing L appropriately, you can capture the typical dependence horizon of your returns or signals.

You then:

- Recompute your strategy's performance on each bootstrap series.
- Use the variation across bootstrap samples to form confidence intervals for metrics like mean return, Sharpe ratio, or maximum drawdown.

Stationary and circular bootstraps

The basic block bootstrap generates series that may have visible discontinuities at block boundaries. More advanced variants soften these issues:

- **Stationary bootstrap.** Blocks have random lengths drawn from a geometric distribution with mean L. At each step, with some probability you continue the current block; with the complementary probability you start a new block at a random location. This creates overlapping blocks of varying length and tends to produce smoother resampled series.
- **Circular bootstrap.** You imagine the time series as arranged on a circle, so that after the last observation you return to the first. Blocks that "wrap around" the end are allowed. This avoids the edge bias that arises when later observations are under-sampled.

These refinements all aim at the same goal: re-create surrogate time series that "look like" the original in terms of dependence and distribution, and then measure how your performance metric varies across such surrogates.

Choosing block length

Block length is the key tuning parameter. If blocks are too short, dependence is broken and the bootstrap underestimates variability. If blocks are too long, the number of effectively independent pieces is small and estimates become noisy.

A practical approach is:

- Relate L to your holding period and the autocorrelation structure of returns or signals. For a strategy with an average holding period of 5 days and noticeable correlation out to 10 days, you might start with L between 10 and 20 days.
- Perform sensitivity checks: compute bootstrap confidence intervals for several plausible L values. If your conclusion (e.g.,

"Sharpe is distinguishable from zero") hinges on a very specific L, be cautious.

Combining Cross-Validation and Resampling

Time-series cross-validation and block bootstraps play complementary roles:

- T-CV explores how performance varies across *time and regimes*.
- Block bootstrap explores how performance varies across *alternative realizations* of similar time series.

A robust validation workflow often layers them:

1. Use blocked or rolling T-CV to define a set of realistic train/test splits and obtain fold-level performance metrics.
2. For each test fold (or for the overall concatenated test path), apply a block bootstrap to estimate confidence intervals for the key metrics.
3. Examine both sources of variability: across time (fold to fold) and across resamples (within each fold).

The resulting picture is richer than either method alone. For example:

- If the mean Sharpe across folds is moderate but every fold's bootstrap interval includes zero, the edge is statistically weak.
- If Sharpe is statistically significant within each fold but deteriorates steadily in later folds, the edge may be real but decaying.
- If performance is highly regime-dependent (great in some folds, terrible in others), you may need regime-switching logic or to restrict deployment to environments where the strategy historically worked.

Walk-Forward Analysis: A Practitioner's Pattern

In industry, many practitioners use "walk-forward analysis" as a concrete implementation of time-series cross-validation that closely matches live trading.

A generic walk-forward pattern looks like this:

1. Choose a training window (e.g., last 3 years) and an evaluation step (e.g., 1 month).
2. Starting from some initial date:
    - Train the model on the current training window.
    - Freeze parameters.
    - Simulate trading over the next step period using only information available up to each decision time.
3. Roll the window forward by the step size and repeat until you reach the end of the sample.
4. Concatenate all step-period results to obtain a continuous equity curve and full distribution of returns, drawdowns, and other metrics.

This is essentially rolling-window T-CV with the additional discipline that you only tune or refit the model at predefined re-estimation dates, just as you would in production. It forces you to think through practical issues such as:

- How often can you reasonably re-estimate parameters?
- How do you handle estimation lag for slow-moving inputs (e.g., quarterly fundamentals)?
- What happens when you deploy the model into regimes it has never seen before?

Because walk-forward analysis produces a single, continuous track record, it also interfaces nicely with downstream risk analysis: maximum drawdown, volatility clustering, regime attribution, and so on.

Detecting Regime Shifts and Structural Breaks

One powerful side effect of time-series cross-validation is that it gives you a structured way to look for regime shifts:

- If early folds show strong performance and later folds weak or negative performance, something important changed.
- If performance is high in high-volatility folds and poor in low-volatility folds (or vice versa), the strategy is regime-sensitive.

You can formalize this by:

- Plotting fold-level Sharpe ratios, hit rates, or other metrics over calendar time.
- Tagging folds by macro or market states (e.g., "crisis," "QE expansion," "rising rates") and comparing performance across states.
- Looking for structural breaks: points in time where the distribution of fold-level returns appears to shift.

When you find such behavior, it should feed back into model design:

- You might restrict deployment to regimes where the edge is strongest.
- You might design explicit regime indicators and condition the strategy on them.
- Or you may conclude that the pattern you thought you discovered was a product of a specific historical era and is unlikely to generalize.

From Point Estimates to Distributions

The unifying idea behind all of these techniques is conceptual: stop thinking of model performance as a single number. In a world of dependent, non-stationary financial data, performance is inherently a random path that will evolve as regimes change and as your signal decays.

Time-series cross-validation and resampling are tools for approximating the distribution of that random path:

- across different launch dates,
- across different market environments,
- across different plausible realizations of returns that share the same structure as the past.

By embracing that distributional view, you become less vulnerable to the most seductive failure mode in quantitative finance: believing that a single, pretty backtest tells you what will happen next.

3.3 Multiple Testing and Hyperparameter Discipline

The previous sections focused on getting the *structure* of validation right in a time-series setting: respect temporal order, avoid leakage, and use time-aware cross-validation and resampling to understand how performance varies across regimes.

Even with all that in place, a quieter, more insidious problem remains: you will almost certainly test many ideas. You will vary features, model classes, hyperparameters, trading universes, and cost assumptions. You will rerun backtests after small tweaks. Each of these is a separate statistical trial. The more trials you run, the more likely you are to find something that looks impressive *purely by chance*.

This section explains how multiple testing and hyperparameter search inflate false discoveries, and it presents a set of tools—Bonferroni-style corrections, false discovery rate (FDR) control, nested cross-validation, and lockbox test sets—to keep you honest.

The Hidden Cost of Many Experiments

Imagine a researcher who runs a single backtest of a strategy whose true expected return is zero. If she uses a conventional significance threshold (say 5%), there is a 5% chance she will see a spuriously good result that passes her threshold just by luck.

Now imagine she runs 100 such backtests, each with a different variation:

- 10 different lookback windows,
- 5 different volatility targets,
- 2 cost assumptions,
- across multiple universes or weighting schemes.

Even if *none* of these variants has a real edge, the probability that at least one will look significant at the 5% level grows with the number of trials. Intuitively, if you flip enough fair coins, you will eventually see a long streak of heads.

This is the multiple testing problem: as the number of hypotheses grows, the chance that you falsely declare at least one of them to be promising (a "false positive") explodes, unless you adjust your criteria.

In quant research, the problem is especially severe because:

- Many experiments are informal and undocumented ("let's just see what happens if we add this filter").
- Results are selectively remembered (you keep the attractive plots, forget the ugly ones).
- Hyperparameter tuning is often treated as a separate, benign activity, when in reality it is a systematic search over many correlated models.

If you do not explicitly control for multiple testing, your research notebook full of "good" backtests is largely a catalog of lucky draws.

From Single-Test to Multiple-Test Thinking

When you evaluate a single strategy variation, traditional hypothesis testing focuses on the chance of a false positive for that one test (Type I error). In multiple testing, the object of interest shifts to:

- The probability of at least one false positive among all tests.
- The proportion of discovered "winners" that are actually false (false discovery rate).

There are two broad families of corrections:

- Family-wise error rate (FWER) control keeps the probability of *any* false positive below a chosen level (e.g., 5%). This is conservative.
- False discovery rate (FDR) control allows some false positives but tries to keep their *proportion* among the selected strategies small on average. This is often more appropriate in exploratory research.

To ground this in practice, think of each candidate model or strategy as a hypothesis:

"Model i has a positive expected risk-adjusted return after costs."

You compute some performance statistic (e.g., Sharpe ratio) and translate it into a p-value or similar measure of evidence. Multiple testing corrections then tell you how to adjust your decision thresholds when you have many such hypotheses on the table.

Simple but Conservative: Bonferroni and Relatives

The Bonferroni correction is conceptually the simplest FWER control method. If you are willing to accept an overall 5% chance of making any false positive among M tests, you require that each individual test be significant at level $0.05/M$.

For example:

- If you run 10 independent tests, each must pass a 0.5% threshold to keep the overall chance of any false positive below 5%.

- If you run 100 tests, each must pass a 0.05% threshold.

This is often harsh in quant settings, because:

- Tests are not independent; variations of the same strategy share trades and cash flows.
- Genuine signals are typically weak; demanding extremely small p-values makes it hard to detect them.

Nonetheless, Bonferroni and similar corrections (like Holm's step-down procedure) serve two important roles:

- They emphasize the basic geometry of the problem: if you search enough, you should be skeptical of moderate-looking evidence.
- They can be applied in small, well-defined testing families (e.g., a handful of clearly distinct strategy concepts) where conservatism is acceptable.

In many exploratory projects, however, you may test dozens or hundreds of related variations. In such cases, FDR control offers a more balanced approach.

False Discovery Rate: Accepting Some Noise

The false discovery rate (FDR) is the expected fraction of false positives among the strategies you decide to keep. Instead of trying to prevent *any* false positive, you aim to ensure that, say, at most 20% of your chosen strategies are spurious in expectation.

One widely used procedure is the Benjamini-Hochberg (BH) method. In broad terms:

- Compute p-values for all M candidate strategies or models.
- Sort these from smallest to largest: $p_{(1)} \leq p_{(2)} \leq \cdots \leq p_{(M)}$.
- Choose a desired FDR level q (e.g., 10% or 20%).

- Find the largest index k such that

$$p_{(k)} \leq \frac{k}{M}q.$$

- Declare all hypotheses with $p_{(i)} \leq p_{(k)}$ (for $i \leq k$) as discoveries.

Intuitively, as you move down the ordered list, you allow larger p-values, but you only keep going as long as the cumulative false discovery budget is not blown. The factor k/M reflects the fact that if you are selecting many strategies, you assign yourself a correspondingly stricter standard at the margin.

FDR control fits exploratory quant research better than FWER because:

- You often expect that only a small fraction of all tested ideas have genuine edge.
- You are usually more concerned that the *portfolio* of chosen strategies is not dominated by noise than that a single noisy strategy sneaks in.

Of course, applying FDR in practice requires that you can:

- Define the "family" of tests clearly (e.g., all backtests in a particular research project).
- Compute reasonably calibrated p-values or equivalent measures (using, for example, block bootstraps on time-series data).

The essential point is conceptual: whenever you are evaluating many variations, you should consciously decide whether you are aiming to control the chance of any false positive (FWER) or the average proportion of false positives among your selected models (FDR). Either is better than pretending you only ran one test.

Hyperparameter Search as Multiple Testing

Hyperparameters—regularization strengths, learning rates, tree depths, lookback windows, and risk-target levels—are often tuned by searching across grids or using automated methods like random search or Bayesian optimization. Each hyperparameter setting corresponds to a different model. Evaluating them on the same validation data is, statistically, another multiple testing problem.

For example, suppose you try 50 different combinations of:

- Lookback window: 20, 60, 120, or 252 days.
- Regularization parameter: 5 values.
- Maximum tree depth: several options.

Your validation procedure effectively promotes the model that happens to look best on that particular validation set. Even if all hyperparameter combinations have the same true predictive power, the one you choose will have an optimistically biased performance estimate on the validation data.

Two consequences follow:

- Reported validation performance is too high; you have "tuned to noise."
- The chosen hyperparameters may be unstable: small changes in the validation sample can lead to very different optimal settings.

The more aggressively you search, the worse the bias becomes. Sophisticated search algorithms like Bayesian optimization can *amplify* this effect by homing in on regions of the hyperparameter space that happen to look especially good on the current data, which may be pure noise.

To maintain integrity, you must treat hyperparameter tuning as *part of* your experimental pipeline, not as a harmless separate step.

Nested Cross-Validation: Separating Tuning from Testing

Nested cross-validation (nested CV) is a principled way to insulate your final performance estimate from the noise induced by hyperparameter search.

The idea is to introduce two layers:

- **Inner loop** used for hyperparameter selection and model choice.
- **Outer loop** used for final, unbiased performance evaluation.

The protocol looks like this in a time-series setting:

1. Define a set of *outer* train/test splits that respect time (for example, blocked or rolling time-series CV folds).
2. For each outer fold:
   (a) Use the outer training period as the universe for an *inner* cross-validation procedure. Within this period:
      - Split the data into inner training and validation segments (again respecting time).
      - For each candidate hyperparameter configuration, evaluate performance across inner folds.
      - Apply your model-selection rule (e.g., pick the configuration with highest mean Sharpe ratio or apply FDR corrections across configurations).

   (b) Once the best configuration is chosen on inner folds, *refit* the model on the entire outer training period using those hyperparameters.

   (c) Evaluate this refitted model on the outer test period *only once*.
3. Aggregate performance across outer folds to obtain your final estimate and distribution of performance.

Critically, the outer test periods are never used to select or tune hyperparameters. They see only the final model, complete with all time-series-aware tuning decisions already baked in. This separation means that the outer test results reflect true out-of-sample performance, including all the noise and overfitting tendencies that occurred during tuning.

Nested CV can be computationally expensive, but the conceptual clarity it brings is invaluable. It turns the outer loop into a realistic rehearsal of production: you observe history up to a certain point, conduct your research (inner loop) using only that history, freeze your model, and then see how it performs in the next period.

Lockbox Sets: The One-Time Final Exam

Even nested CV can be gamed if you repeatedly look at the outer-fold results and make high-level research decisions based on them (e.g., discarding lines of research that do poorly and focusing on those that do well). Over time, you end up effectively tuning to the outer folds as well.

To protect against this, many practitioners designate a *lockbox* set: a portion of data that is set aside at the very beginning of the project and is not touched—in any way—until the end.

Characteristics of a lockbox:

- It is typically a contiguous time block at the end of your sample, representing the most recent history.
- It is excluded from all modeling, tuning, feature engineering, and cross-validation during development.
- It is used exactly once, at the end, to evaluate the fully frozen research protocol.

You can think of the lockbox as a final exam under proctored conditions: you only get one attempt, and you cannot rewrite the exam after you see the grade.

In practice:

1. Split your data into:
    - Development set: early to mid-history, used for all exploratory work, nested CV, multiple testing corrections, and model selection.

- Lockbox set: later history, kept untouched.

2. Conduct your entire research program on the development set. This includes:

    - Trying many ideas, applying FDR or other multiple-testing controls.
    - Using nested CV for hyperparameter search.
    - Deciding on the final model architecture, features, and risk controls.

3. Once the protocol is frozen, open the lockbox:

    - Apply the chosen model and rules exactly as they would have been applied in real time, using only information available at each decision date.
    - Generate a lockbox performance report (returns, drawdowns, etc.).

If the lockbox performance is broadly consistent with your development-set expectations, you have at least passed one strong test against overfitting. If it collapses, you have evidence that your validation and multiple-testing controls were insufficient.

Visual Blueprint: Nested Tuning with a Lockbox

Figure summarizes the interplay between inner tuning, outer evaluation, and the final lockbox test in a single flow diagram.

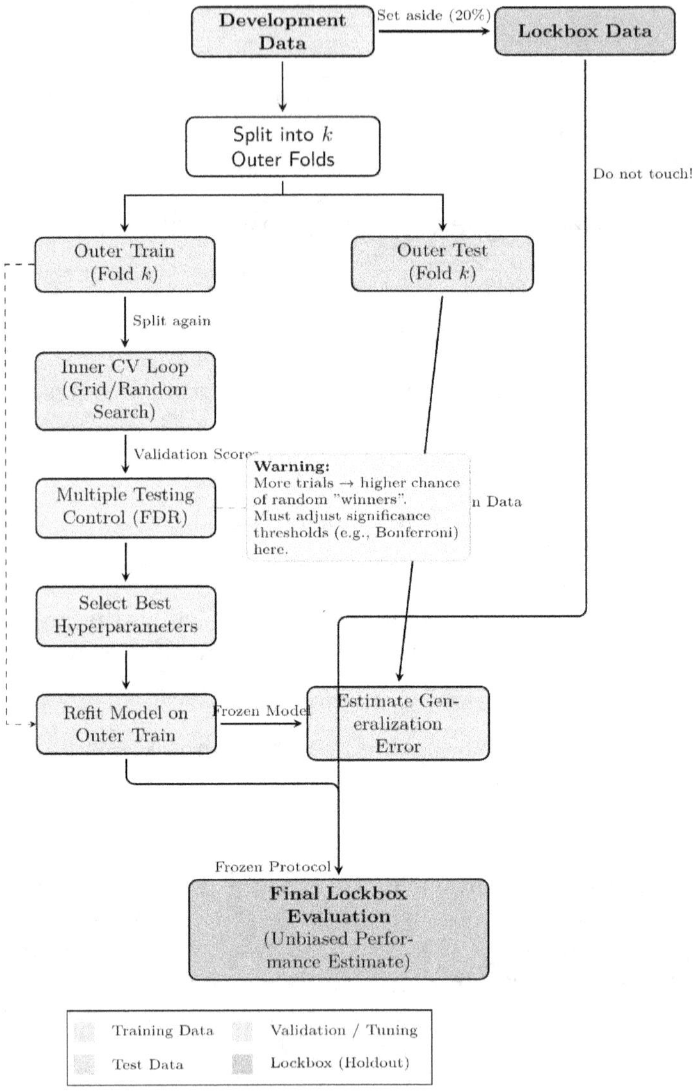
Development Data
Set aside (20%)
Lockbox Data
Split into k Outer Folds
Do not touch!
Outer Train (Fold k)
Outer Test (Fold k)
Split again
Inner CV Loop (Grid/Random Search)
Validation Score
Warning:
More trials → higher chance of random "winners".
Must adjust significance thresholds (e.g., Bonferroni) here.
n Data
Multiple Testing Control (FDR)
Select Best Hyperparameters
Refit Model on Outer Train
Frozen Model
Estimate Generalization Error
Frozen Protocol
Final Lockbox Evaluation (Unbiased Performance Estimate)
Training Data
Validation / Tuning
Test Data
Lockbox (Holdout)

Practical Workflows and Research Hygiene

The tools above are most effective when embedded in disciplined workflows. A few practical habits can dramatically reduce your exposure to overfit discoveries.

Pre-register hyperparameter ranges and test budgets

Before you see any performance results in a new project, write down:

- The range of hyperparameters you intend to search (e.g., learning rates, depths, lookbacks).
- The approximate number of candidate models you will evaluate.
- The multiple-testing control you will apply (e.g., "We will cap the family-wise error at 5% via Holm-Bonferroni across these 20 concept-level tests" or "We will control FDR at 10% across all variations of this family.").

You do not need a fully formal pre-registration protocol, but even a rough "research plan" note forces you to confront the scale of your search and how you plan to adjust for it. Revising the plan midstream is acceptable, but revisions should be explicit and justified, not silent moves of the goalposts.

Reuse validation folds across related ideas

If you test multiple, closely related models (e.g., different transformations of the same factor), use the *same* validation folds and evaluation protocol for all of them. This has two benefits:

- It reduces the effective dimensionality of the multiple-testing problem, because variations are more directly comparable.
- It exposes how sensitive each idea is to particular folds and regimes.

Ad hoc changes to validation windows or metrics to "help" a struggling idea are clear red flags.

Maintain a "model cemetery"

Keep a log of all serious model variants and strategies you have tested, not just the ones that worked. For each entry, record:

- The date, data period, and universe used.
- The concept and key hyperparameters.
- The validation protocol and performance summary.

A model cemetery serves several purposes:

- It provides an honest picture of how many experiments have been run, supporting appropriate multiple-testing adjustments.
- It prevents "zombie" ideas from resurfacing without acknowledging their prior failures.
- It helps diagnose research biases ("We have tried 30 mean-reversion variants and only remember the one that worked in 2013-2015.").

Look for signs of overfit tuning

Several qualitative patterns are strong warnings that hyperparameter search has overfit to noise:

- **Fragile optima:** Performance peaks sharply at a very specific parameter combination and deteriorates quickly when you move away from it. Robust edges tend to produce broader plateaus of reasonably good performance, not razor-thin spikes.
- **Chasing episodes:** The chosen hyperparameters seem tailor-made to exploit one particular historical episode (for example, a specific crisis or bubble) and perform poorly elsewhere.
- **Instability across folds:** The "best" hyperparameters differ wildly from outer fold to outer fold and seem to track local noise rather than a consistent pattern.

When you see these patterns, tighten your discipline: reduce the search space, apply stricter multiple-testing controls, or revert to simpler, more transparent models.

From Anecdotes to Evidence

Multiple testing and hyperparameter discipline are ultimately about a cultural shift in how you interpret backtests:

- A single, impressive backtest is an *anecdote*.
- A family of backtests, rigorously adjusted for the number of trials and accompanied by uncertainty estimates, is *evidence*.

By explicitly counting your experiments, controlling FWER or FDR where appropriate, insulating tuning from testing through nested cross-validation, and preserving an untouched lockbox for the final exam, you convert a laboratory full of tempting stories into a smaller set of genuinely credible candidates.

This discipline does not eliminate failure in live trading—markets change, and signals decay. But it greatly increases the likelihood that when a model fails, it fails for real economic reasons, not because you were fooled by the combinatorial lottery of overfit research.

3.4 Credible Backtest Design and Simulation

The earlier sections of this chapter established how to validate models on time-series data: respect temporal order, avoid leakage, account for multiple testing, and insulate tuning from final evaluation. In this section we move from *estimating* performance to *simulating* it in a way that is as close as possible to real trading.

A good backtest is not a marketing slide. It is a dry run of the production engine under realistic constraints. That means:

- Using point-in-time data that reflects what was actually knowable at each decision date.
- Respecting liquidity, borrow and capital constraints.

- Modeling transaction costs, slippage, and market impact explicitly.
- Freezing parameters and decision rules when you claim they were frozen.

This section defines what it means for a backtest to be *tradable* and walks through a modular architecture for credible simulations.

What Makes a Backtest Tradable?

A backtest is tradable if, at any point on its simulated equity curve, a competent trader could have reproduced the portfolio with the information and resources actually available at that time. That deceptively simple statement implies several concrete requirements.

Point-in-time information

All inputs must reflect the state of the world as of the decision time:

- **Prices and returns** must be free of look-ahead. If you trade at the open using yesterday's close, you may not use the current day's close to decide what to do.
- **Fundamental data** (earnings, balance sheets, analyst estimates) must be timestamped with their true availability dates, including reporting delays, restatements, and data vendor lags.
- **Corporate actions** (splits, dividends, mergers) must be accounted for using split-adjusted or total-return series that do not "rewrite history" with information known only later.

Using a modern data extract that has been backfilled with future corrections, or that omits delisted names, produces the familiar pathologies of look-ahead and survivorship bias. In a tradable backtest, you consciously choose a point in time—say, 31 March 2014—and reconstruct the investable universe and all signals using only data that existed then.

Cost- and liquidity-awareness

A backtest that ignores trading costs and liquidity is merely a demonstration of theoretical predictability, not of tradable profit.

Credible simulations must:

- Apply realistic **transaction costs**: commissions, fees, bid-ask spreads.
- Include **slippage**: the difference between the decision price (e.g., mid-quote at signal time) and the actual fill price.
- Approximate **market impact**: the price movement caused by your own orders, especially for large trades in less liquid names.
- Enforce **size limits**: do not trade more volume than the market could plausibly absorb (for instance, cap participation as a fraction of average daily volume).

The aim is not to get every micro-detail perfect, but to be directionally realistic and to err on the conservative side.

Parameter-frozen protocols

At some point in the research process, you freeze:

- The model architecture and feature definitions.
- Hyperparameter settings.
- Cost models and universe definitions.
- Risk and portfolio-construction rules.

From that "freeze date" forward, the protocol must be applied mechanically, without peeking at future outcomes to refine it. In a tradable backtest, any claim of live-like performance (including simulated out-of-sample periods such as nested CV outer folds or lockbox tests) must refer to a period in which the protocol was already fixed.

Without parameter freezing, you are constantly adapting the model to the most recent data, which is another form of leakage.

Requirements for a Credible Pipeline

Before we build the architecture, it is useful to summarize the core requirements for a credible backtest pipeline:

1. **Point-in-time data:** All data sources are aligned to their as-of dates, with listing and delisting histories, corporate actions, and vendor lags respected.

2. **Information-consistent signals:** Signals are computed using only data available at the decision time and with appropriate lookback windows.

3. **Modular stack:** Alpha, portfolio construction, risk management, and execution are distinct layers with clear interfaces.

4. **Realistic trading mechanics:** Order generation, queuing, and fills approximate how orders would be executed in the market.

5. **Costs and constraints:** Transaction costs, impact, liquidity limits, borrow constraints, and regulatory or mandate constraints are enforced.

6. **Parameter freeze and lockbox:** The final backtest reflects a frozen research protocol evaluated on data not used in its design.

We now turn to a layered architecture that helps you enforce these requirements in practice.

A Layered Backtest Architecture

A modular, layered design not only makes your backtests easier to maintain; it also makes it easier to reason about where assumptions enter and to ensure that each layer respects time and information flow.

Figure presents a schematic of a credible backtest pipeline, from raw point-in-time data to execution and performance reporting.

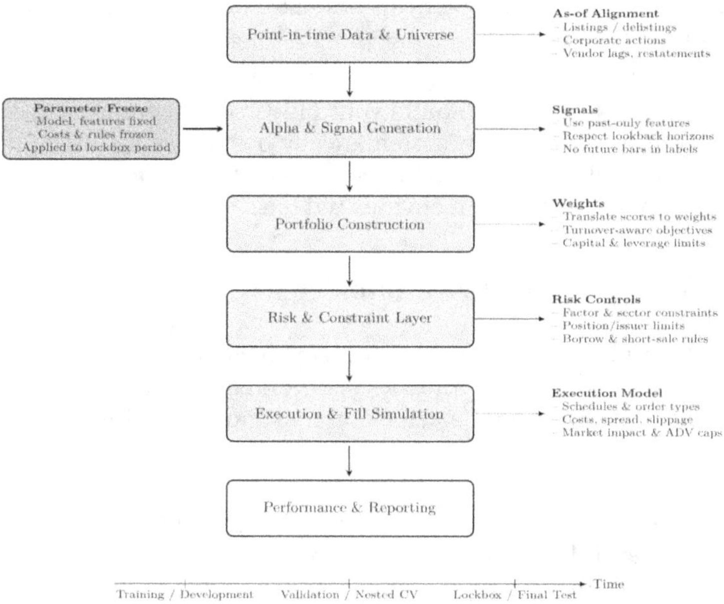

We now examine these layers in more detail.

Point-in-Time Data and Universe Construction

Everything begins with data. If the foundation is flawed, no amount of clever modeling can repair it.

Listings, delistings, and survivorship

A credible universe:

- Includes securities that were actually available to trade at each date, based on listing and delisting histories.
- Removes securities from the universe after they delist, are acquired, or otherwise become untradeable, with appropriate treatment of final cashflows.

- Does *not* silently exclude firms that later failed or were acquired at low valuations.

Survivorship bias, where you build your universe only from securities that survived to the present, systematically overstates historical performance and understates risk. A backtest that never holds a company that later went bankrupt is an obvious red flag.

Corporate actions and price adjustment

To avoid phantom jumps in your returns, you will typically work with adjusted prices that account for stock splits and dividends. The critical detail is that the adjustment mechanism must not leak future information. For example:

- On a split date, the past price history is rescaled. Your backtest must treat this as a local event, not as a redefinition of all past prices from the vantage point of the distant future.
- Dividend adjustments must be such that you can reconstruct the pre-dividend price path that would have been seen in real time, while also correctly crediting cashflows to the portfolio on ex-dividend and payment dates.

The safest approach is to work from raw data (unadjusted trades and quotes plus corporate action events) and build your own adjusted series with explicit rules. If you rely on vendor-adjusted data, you must understand their conventions.

Fundamentals and data lags

Fundamental data (earnings, book values, analyst estimates) often arrives with delays and is subsequently revised. In a credibly simulated backtest:

- Each observation has an as-of date, which may be later than the fiscal period end.

- You only use fundamental values that were published and available by the decision date, possibly with vendor-specific lags.
- Revisions and restatements are handled as new information, not retroactively applied to past periods.

Failing to account for data lags has the same effect as using tomorrow's newspaper to trade yesterday's close.

Alpha and Signal Generation

The alpha layer transforms raw, point-in-time data into quantitative signals that express your forecasts or preferences.

Lookbacks and horizons

Two time scales must be respected:

- **Lookback horizon:** how far back you look to compute a signal (e.g., 12-month momentum, 10-day volatility).
- **Prediction horizon:** the period over which the signal is intended to forecast returns or risks (e.g., 1 day, 1 month).

Signals must be computed using only data within the lookback window that ends at the decision time. Any use of future returns, even indirectly (such as realized volatility measured from t to $t+1$ when trading at t), creates leakage.

Signal stability and refresh frequency

In a tradable backtest, signal updates should reflect realistic operational practice:

- End-of-day strategies may recompute signals once per day using the full close data.

- Intraday strategies might update signals at specific bar boundaries (e.g., every 5 minutes).

If your backtest recomputes signals using the entire day's trade history and then pretends you acted at the open, you are implicitly granting yourself clairvoyance.

Portfolio Construction

Portfolio construction translates signals into target positions.

From scores to weights

Common approaches include:

- Rank-based schemes (e.g., long top decile, short bottom decile).
- Mean-variance optimizers and risk-parity allocations.
- Heuristics that cap weights by volatility or liquidity.

Whatever the method, a credible backtest should:

- Limit concentration in single names or sectors.
- Reflect leverage and margin constraints.
- Control turnover, since high turnover amplifies trading costs.

Portfolio construction and signal generation are tightly linked: an alpha that looks attractive in isolation may be impractical when combined with realistic constraints.

Turnover and rebalance discipline

Define explicit rebalance rules:

- At what times are portfolios re-optimized (daily close, weekly, monthly)?
- Do you allow intra-day rebalancing in response to market moves?
- How do you handle partial fills or leftovers from previous days?

A backtest that implicitly assumes you can instantly jump from one target portfolio to another without considering intermediate states or execution constraints is unrealistic.

Risk and Constraint Layer

The risk layer supervises exposures that are not directly encoded in the alpha model but are essential for tradability and mandate compliance.

Factor and sector exposures

Even if your alpha is designed to be market-neutral, in practice you must:

- Monitor and limit exposures to market beta, size, value, momentum, sectors, countries, and other known drivers.
- Adjust portfolios to stay within predefined exposure bands (e.g., market beta between -0.1 and 0.1).

These adjustments often override pure alpha recommendations, and a realistic backtest must include them.

Position and issuer constraints

Common constraints include:

- Maximum position size as a fraction of portfolio NAV.
- Maximum ownership as a fraction of free float.

- Limits on exposure to single issuers or related groups.

These constraints should be enforced at each rebalance in simulation, just as they would be in production.

Shorting and borrow constraints

Short-selling is not free:

- Some securities are hard to borrow; others are impossible.
- Borrow costs vary and must be debited against returns.
- Recall risk (lenders demanding their shares back) can force unwanted closes.

Many naïve backtests treat shorts as symmetric to longs. A credible simulation at least:

- Applies realistic borrow costs (possibly as a function of utilization or short interest).
- Limits short positions to assets with reliable borrow availability.
- Penalizes crowded shorts more heavily.

Execution and Fill Simulation

Even with perfect alpha and immaculate portfolio construction, poor execution can erase any edge.

Order generation

At each rebalance time, the backtest must:

- Compute trade lists: the difference between current and target positions.

- Encode order sizes and directions (buy/sell, open/close, reduce/increase).
- Decide on order types and timing (market, limit, VWAP schedules, etc.).

These decisions can materially affect realized performance, especially for large or illiquid orders.

Costs, spreads, and slippage

A minimal execution model includes:

- **Commission**: fixed or per-share fees.
- **Bid-ask spread**: crossing the spread incurs half-spread costs per trade.
- **Slippage**: additional price movement between signal and execution, often modeled as a function of volatility, trade size, and market conditions.

More sophisticated models introduce **market impact**:

- Estimated as a function of participation rate (trade size relative to average daily volume), volatility, and existing order-book depth.
- Applied as a penalty to effective execution price.

Regardless of complexity, conservative assumptions are preferable. When in doubt, assume costs are slightly worse than historical averages, not better.

Liquidity and participation limits

A model that suggests buying 50% of a day's volume in a thinly traded stock is not tradable. Your simulator should enforce:

- Maximum participation per security per day (e.g., no more than 10% of recent average daily volume).
- Lower participation caps in the presence of volatility spikes or unusual order-book conditions.

If the model's target weights would violate these limits, the simulator should either scale down positions or accept that some target moves cannot be achieved within the step.

Performance and Reporting

The final layer computes returns, drawdowns, and other metrics from the simulated fills and positions.

Cashflows and path dependency

Performance should reflect:

- All cashflows: trade proceeds, dividends, coupons, borrow fees, financing costs.
- Realistic compounding: reinvestment or withdrawal policies.
- Exact timing of returns (intraday, daily, monthly), as appropriate for your strategy.

Backtest reports should emphasize full-path metrics (e.g., maximum drawdown, worst rolling 12-month period) rather than just average returns.

Attribution and diagnostics

A credible backtest makes it easy to ask:

- How much performance comes from alpha versus leverage or directional exposure?

- How much is eaten by trading costs and borrow fees?
- Which names or sectors contributed most to risk and return?

These diagnostics help you separate structural flaws (e.g., too much cost) from genuine but possibly weak alpha.

Integrating Parameter Freezing and Lockboxes

The architectural layers described above apply both during development and during final evaluation. The difference is:

- **During development**, you are free to modify the alpha, portfolio, risk, and execution logic, as long as changes are validated with the time-aware and multiple-testing protocols discussed in earlier sections.
- **After the parameter freeze date**, all layers are fixed. You apply the exact same code and configuration to the lockbox period, with no further tuning.

In practice:

1. Use your development data to design and validate the full pipeline, including cost and liquidity models, via nested CV and careful multiple testing.
2. Once satisfied, freeze the protocol and document it.
3. Run the lockbox backtest by feeding point-in-time data for the lockbox period into the already-frozen stack.
4. Treat the resulting performance as your best unbiased estimate of tradable behavior up to that point.

If lockbox results are materially worse than development-stage expectations, that is a signal to re-examine your assumptions and validation process, not to tweak the model to "fix" the lockbox. At most, you may learn lessons for the next research cycle.

From Slides to Engines

A marketing backtest is a picture designed to persuade. A credible backtest is an engine designed to withstand scrutiny. It is:

- Built on point-in-time data and realistic trading mechanics.
- Structured as a modular pipeline whose assumptions are explicit and testable.
- Validated with time-aware splits, time-series cross-validation, and honest multiple-testing controls.
- Evaluated on a lockbox period with frozen parameters.

Such a backtest will not always produce exciting results; many ideas will die in this more demanding environment. That is precisely the point. By insisting that simulated performance be plausibly tradable, you filter out models whose apparent success is due to data leakage, cost blindness, or overfitting to historical quirks, leaving a smaller set of candidates that have earned the right to face real markets.

Chapter 4

Overfitting Theory and Diagnostics

Most quants meet overfitting as a moral warning-"don't torture the data"-but not as a measurable, manageable risk. This chapter turns overfitting into something you can model, test, and price in basis points. We will connect model flexibility, sample size, and search intensity to inflated Sharpe ratios, then bring in information criteria, probabilistic Sharpe adjustments, and the Probability of Backtest Overfitting to ask a sharper question: not "does my backtest look good?" but "how likely is this performance to survive contact with the future?"

4.1 Model Complexity and Bias–Variance Mechanics

In previous chapters, we treated a trading strategy as a mapping from information (prices, fundamentals, order book features, macro variables) to positions and returns. We also saw that historical backtests provide only a noisy glimpse of how well that mapping may work in the future. In this section we make that idea more precise by introducing *model complexity* and linking it to the classic bias–variance trade-off. Our goal is to understand why, in typical financial data sets, increasing complexity and running large parameter searches almost inevitably manufactures apparent edge.

What Do We Mean by "Model Complexity" in Trading?

In statistics, a model is more complex if it can fit a wider variety of patterns. In trading, we usually care less about formal definitions and more about practical sources of flexibility—the knobs and switches that allow a strategy to mold itself to a specific backtest.

Several dimensions of complexity matter in quantitative strategies:

1. **Number of explicit parameters.** These are the obvious degrees of freedom:
   - Lookback windows (20-day vs. 60-day momentum).
   - Thresholds (enter trade if score > 1.5).
   - Stop-loss and take-profit levels.
   - Signals weights in a linear combination.

   Each extra parameter increases the number of possible behaviors the strategy can express.

2. **Functional flexibility.** Even with the same number of parameters, some functional forms are more flexible than others:
   - A linear regression with one predictor is less flexible than a neural network using the same predictor but with multiple hidden units.
   - A simple moving-average crossover is less flexible than a tree model that splits on many interacting conditions.

   Non-linearities, interaction terms, and regime switches all increase functional flexibility.

3. **Search breadth over specifications.** Complexity is not only "inside" one model. It also comes from how many alternative formulations you try:

    - Different sets of predictors (price-only vs. price + volume + macro).
    - Different transformations (levels vs. logs vs. vol-adjusted).
    - Different portfolio construction rules (equal-weight vs. risk-parity vs. volatility targeting).

    Even if each individual model is simple, exploring hundreds of variants produces a very large effective search space.

4. **Hidden filters and conditions.** Real research often adds filters:

    - Only trade when VIX is below/above some level.
    - Skip trades near major announcements.
    - Require minimum liquidity or spread conditions.

    Each filter slices the data in another way and contributes to overall flexibility.

5. **Time segmentation and regime switches.** Allowing parameters or rules to change across subperiods or regimes (crisis vs. normal, high vs. low volatility) magnifies the number of ways the model can fit past data.

We can summarize these ideas informally by saying:

> A trading strategy is more complex when it can adapt to a greater variety of return paths by tuning its parameters, structure, or filters.

This is powerful, because a flexible strategy can in principle capture subtle real patterns. But it is also dangerous, because the same flexibility will eagerly chase patterns that are just noise.

Error Decomposition: Bias and Variance in a Trading Context

To understand why complexity cuts both ways, we use the bias–variance framework. Consider an unknown data-generating process that maps information X_t (features at time t) to a next-period return r_{t+1}:

$$r_{t+1} = f^*(X_t) + \varepsilon_{t+1},$$

where f^* is the true (and unknown) mapping, and ε_{t+1} is noise—unpredictable shocks.

Our model builds an estimate $\hat{f}(X_t)$ of $f^*(X_t)$ using finite historical data. The prediction error at a point X can be decomposed into:

- **Bias:** Systematic difference between the model's average prediction and the truth.
- **Variance:** Sensitivity of the model's prediction to the particular sample of data we happened to see.

In words:

- A *high-bias* model is too rigid to learn the true relationship, even with a lot of data. In trading, an example is a naive constant-mean model applied to a world with genuine cross-sectional return differences: it ignores real signal structure.
- A *high-variance* model is so flexible that its fitted parameters change dramatically when the data sample changes. In trading, this shows up as a strategy whose optimal parameters are very unstable across time windows, or whose backtest equity curve moves from stellar to disastrous with only minor specification changes.

The total expected out-of-sample error can be thought of (informally) as:

$$\text{Total error} \approx \text{Bias}^2 + \text{Variance} + \text{Irreducible noise}.$$

The irreducible noise comes from ε_{t+1}—risk that is in principle unpredictable. In financial markets, this noise term is often large relative to any predictable component, especially at high frequencies and short horizons.

How Complexity Trades Off Bias and Variance

As we allow a model to become more complex, two things tend to happen:

1. **Bias decreases.** A more flexible model can approximate a wider range of relationships. With enough data, it can get closer to f^*.
2. **Variance increases.** A more flexible model can also fit quirks specific to one sample: random spikes, temporary correlations, particular crisis episodes. Different samples yield different fitted parameters, and predictions become unstable.

This leads to the typical story: as complexity increases from a very simple baseline, total error first declines (because bias drops faster than variance rises), then hits a minimum, and then increases again once variance dominates.

The key point for quants is that, because financial data are noisy and often short, the right-hand side—the overfitting regime—arrives much sooner than our intuition suggests.

Why Finance is Especially Vulnerable: Short, Noisy Samples

In many scientific domains, large sample sizes and high signal-to-noise ratios give models room to become more complex before variance becomes fatal. In trading, we face the opposite situation:

- **Few independent observations.** Daily equity returns over 10 years provide about 2,500 data points, but they are strongly autocorrelated through volatility, regimes, and overlapping positions. Effective independent observations are far fewer. At intraday horizons, microstructure noise makes this worse.

- **Low signal-to-noise ratio.** A strategy with a true Sharpe ratio of 0.5 per year has a modest edge compared with daily volatility of 1–2% or more. Over moderate samples, the noise easily masks or mimics such a signal.
- **Non-stationarity.** Market relationships change over time. A strategy that is very well tuned to 2008–2012 crisis dynamics may generalize poorly to 2016–2019, even if it avoids classical statistical overfitting in each subperiod.

These features effectively shrink the usable information content of historical data. When the amount of genuine information is small, even modest model flexibility can push us into the high-variance region where apparent performance improvements are mostly luck.

From Complexity to "Too Good To Be True" Backtests

How does this theory materialize in real research? Consider a stylized example.

Example: A Simple Momentum Strategy

Suppose you start with a simple cross-sectional momentum signal:

- Each month, rank stocks by past k-month return.
- Go long the top decile, short the bottom decile.

You try a few lookbacks: $k \in \{3, 6, 12\}$ months, holding period of 1 month. The resulting annualized backtest Sharpe ratios are:

3-month: 0.7; 6-month: 0.9; 12-month: 0.8.

You choose $k = 6$ months as your preferred specification. Complexity here is modest: a single parameter, a limited search.

Now imagine a more aggressive search:

- Lookbacks k from 1 to 24 months.
- Holding periods from 1 to 6 months.
- Volatility scaling on/off.
- Various filters (e.g., trade only when market is above its 200-day moving average).

You end up with several hundred combinations. It is almost guaranteed that one of them will show an annualized Sharpe of, say, 1.8 or higher, with a smooth equity curve and attractive drawdowns. But we must ask: is that because the underlying idea is truly strong, or because with so much flexibility you have fitted the historical noise?

The bias–variance perspective tells us that:

- We have reduced bias: the richer family of models can approximate a wider range of true dynamics.
- We have greatly increased variance: our chosen best model is now the maximum of many noisy realizations. Its in-sample performance is upwardly biased by selection.

In other words, the backtest Sharpe has become a *highly optimistic* estimator of the true Sharpe.

T-Overfit: Capacity, Search Intensity, and Sample Size

For trading, it is useful to talk about an informal regime we can call *T-overfit*: the point at which the effective capacity of the modeling process, multiplied by the intensity of the specification search, becomes large relative to the available independent observations in the backtest.

Three ingredients drive us into T-overfit:

1. **Effective model capacity.** This includes:

   - The number of explicit parameters.
   - The richness of the functional form (linear vs. deep non-linear).
   - The use of regime switches or time-varying parameters.

2. **Specification search intensity.** How broadly and aggressively we explore:

   - Number of different signal definitions.
   - Number of transformations and filters.
   - Number of portfolio construction and risk overlays.

   Even if each individual model has moderate capacity, a large search over many such models creates substantial effective flexibility.

3. **Available independent observations.** The true number of independent pieces of information:

   - Adjusted for overlapping positions and returns.
   - Adjusted for regime changes and structural breaks.
   - Adjusted for cross-sectional dependencies when trading many correlated assets.

We are in the T-overfit regime when:

> The combined flexibility of the models and the breadth of the search are large compared with the amount of genuine information in the backtest.

In this regime, apparent improvements in in-sample Sharpe, drawdown statistics, or equity-curve smoothness are mostly the result of fitting noise. The true out-of-sample performance of the chosen specification will revert toward that of an average strategy in the tested family, not the in-sample champion.

Practical Signs That You Are in the Overfitting Regime

The theory can feel abstract. Here are practical, observable signals that you are likely on the right-hand side of the bias–variance curve:

1. **Hypersensitivity to minor tweaks.** Small changes in parameters or definitions cause large swings in performance:

    - 19-day vs. 20-day moving average changes Sharpe from 1.5 to 0.4.
    - Slightly different rebalancing days or execution assumptions reverse the sign of the backtest.

    High variance means performance is unstable under small perturbations.

2. **Many filters required to look acceptable.** The core idea performs poorly without an assortment of filters and conditions (market regime filters, volatility filters, event exclusions, etc.), and only looks attractive with a precise combination of them. This suggests that the filters are mainly sculpting noise.

3. **Sharp deterioration under coarse evaluation.** When you:

    - Aggregate returns to lower frequency (weekly or monthly),
    - Or re-estimate performance on slightly shifted sample windows,

    the strategy's Sharpe and equity curve degrade sharply. A genuine underlying edge should survive such coarse-graining; pure noise fits will not.

4. **Track record that is too smooth for the horizon and assets.** For example, a daily strategy on volatile single stocks showing an almost monotonic equity curve with tiny drawdowns over a short sample is a red flag. Because the noise component at such horizons is large, realistic edges will still produce messy paths.

5. **Unstable "optimal" parameters across time.** Re-running your parameter search on rolling or expanding windows yields

wildly different best choices. This indicates that the apparent edge depends heavily on the specific historical slice.

These are not mathematical proofs of overfitting, but they are strong symptoms that variance is dominating and that your modeling process is in a T-overfit regime.

Complexity, Parameter Search, and Inflated Sharpe Ratios

It is helpful to think of Sharpe ratios themselves as random variables. Even if the true Sharpe of a strategy were fixed, any finite-sample estimate will fluctuate due to noise. With N independent observations, the standard error of the annualized Sharpe estimate is roughly proportional to $1/\sqrt{N}$ (ignoring complications like autocorrelation and non-normality). When N is modest—as it usually is in finance—these fluctuations can be substantial.

Now consider the effect of parameter search:

- You evaluate M candidate strategies, each with the same true Sharpe, but each subject to its own sampling noise.
- You select the one with the highest backtest Sharpe.

By construction, the maximum of M noisy estimates will be an upward-biased estimate of the common true Sharpe. The larger M is, the more extreme this bias becomes. Aggressive parameter searches (large M) effectively guarantee that some model will exhibit an impressive in-sample Sharpe, even if no genuine edge exists.

When we add model complexity on top of this (which increases variance further), the problem compounds:

- Complex models have higher variance in their performance estimates.
- Large searches over complex models create a very high chance that the selected winner is mostly a noise-fit.

In later sections we will formalize this intuition with tools such as adjusted Sharpe metrics and the probability of backtest overfitting. For now, the key message is that *complexity plus search equals optimism*: a glossy backtest is often a statement about the researcher's flexibility and persistence, not about the quality of the trading signal.

Rules of Thumb for Staying Out of Trouble

While we will later introduce more formal diagnostics, it is useful to adopt some conservative habits at this stage:

- **Favor simpler specifications that explain most of the effect.** If a simple model and a more complex one deliver similar performance, treat the simpler as superior unless the extra complexity is clearly justified (e.g., by robust economic intuition or strong out-of-sample validation).
- **Limit the breadth of exploratory searches.** Avoid blind grids over large parameter spaces. Start from economically motivated ranges and keep track of how many variations you have tried.
- **Probe stability aggressively.** Routinely:
  - Shift estimation windows.
  - Vary data cleaning conventions.
  - Change rebalancing dates and execution assumptions within realistic bounds.

  If performance is fragile, treat it as suspect.
- **Be wary of short backtests with high Sharpe.** Extremely high in-sample Sharpe ratios over short samples are almost always artifacts of variance and search. A modest Sharpe observed over a long, stable history is usually more credible.
- **Track and penalize hidden complexity.** Count not only explicit parameters but also:
  - Ad-hoc filters,

  - Manually chosen breakpoints,
  - Regime-specific tuning.

  These all expand effective model capacity and move you toward the overfitting regime.

In the next section we will connect these informal ideas to more formal tools, such as information criteria and minimum description length, which provide principled ways to penalize complexity and control overfitting risk.

4.2 Information Criteria and Minimum Description Length

In the previous section we saw how model complexity interacts with bias and variance, and how aggressive specification searches can transform noise into an apparently beautiful equity curve. We now turn to a central practical question: *how complex is too complex?* More precisely, when does an additional parameter, filter, or breakpoint *earn* its keep, and when is it just sculpting noise?

Information criteria and the Minimum Description Length (MDL) principle give us a disciplined answer. Rather than asking which model produces the highest in-sample Sharpe, they ask which model offers the best trade-off between fit and parsimony. In that sense, they are formal tools for implementing the intuition that the right model for trading is the one that explains the data with the *shortest honest description.*

From "Best Fit" to "Best Explanation"

A natural, but naive, approach to model selection is:

> Fit many models and pick the one with the best in-sample performance metric (Sharpe, log-likelihood, mean squared error, or P&L).

As we have already discussed, this rewards complexity and search intensity. A more honest question is:

> Given two models, which one gives a better explanation of the data *without* wasting parameters?

To answer this, we need a score that:

- Rewards models that fit the data well.
- Penalizes models that are needlessly complex.

Information criteria such as the Akaike Information Criterion (AIC) and the Bayesian Information Criterion (BIC) are built exactly on this idea. They start from a measure of fit (a log-likelihood) and subtract a penalty that grows with the number of parameters and, in the case of BIC, with the effective sample size. MDL takes the same idea a step further and rephrases it in terms of how many "bits" it takes to describe the model and its residual errors.

Likelihood and Model Fit in Plain Language

Before introducing AIC and BIC, we need a simple notion of likelihood. Very informally:

- The *likelihood* of a model is a number that tells us how plausible the observed data are under that model.
- A higher likelihood means the model assigns higher probability to what we actually saw.

In practice, we usually work with the log-likelihood, which is just the logarithm of the likelihood. This turns products of probabilities into sums, which is easier to handle.

For a trading strategy, think in the following way:

- Suppose you have a statistical model for returns (or for the strategy's P&L path) with some parameters.

- Once you estimate those parameters from historical data, you can compute how likely it is that such a sequence of returns would have been generated under that model.

A model that fits the data better will generally have a higher log-likelihood. But, as we know from overfitting, simply making the model more flexible—for example, by adding parameters—almost always increases the maximum log-likelihood you can obtain, even if those extra parameters capture only noise.

AIC and BIC respond by saying, in effect:

> We will give you credit for higher log-likelihood, but we will subtract points for every parameter you introduce.

Akaike Information Criterion (AIC): Reward Fit, Penalize Parameters

The Akaike Information Criterion (AIC) is one of the earliest and most widely used information criteria. For a model with k parameters fitted to a sample of size n, its AIC value is constructed as:

AIC = (measure of lack of fit) + (penalty proportional to number of parameters).

In its likelihood form, this is often written (omitting constants) as:

$$\text{AIC} = -2\,(\text{log-likelihood}) + 2k.$$

The constants are not important here; what matters is the structure:

- The first term decreases when the model fits better (higher log-likelihood means smaller -2 times log-likelihood).
- The second term increases as we add parameters.

How to interpret AIC in trading research.

- **Lower AIC is better.** Among a set of candidate models fitted to the same data, the one with the lowest AIC is preferred.
- **Penalizes every extra knob.** Each additional parameter, filter, or breakpoint you introduce effectively costs you a fixed AIC penalty.
- **Favors models that improve fit *enough*.** If a more complex model improves the log-likelihood only slightly, the extra penalty can make its AIC worse (higher), thus favoring the simpler model.

Think of AIC as asking: if you were allowed to transmit the model parameters and then the data residuals to a colleague, how much total information would that require? Extra parameters lengthen the "model description"; better fit shortens the "residual description". AIC approximately balances these two.

Example: Nested trading rules.

Suppose you have two models for daily returns of a strategy:

- Model S (simple): returns depend on a single factor (say, past 1-month momentum).
- Model C (complex): returns depend on the same factor plus three additional technical indicators.

Model C, after fitting, produces a slightly higher in-sample Sharpe and a slightly higher log-likelihood than Model S. However, Model C has three more parameters.

If the improvement in log-likelihood is *not* large enough to compensate for the $2k$ penalty for those extra parameters, then Model S will have a lower AIC and will be preferred. Intuitively, AIC here is saying: the subtle extra contouring of the equity curve bought by those indicators is not enough to justify their added complexity.

Bayesian Information Criterion (BIC): Stricter on Complexity

The Bayesian Information Criterion (BIC) is similar in spirit, but imposes a stronger penalty for complexity, especially as the sample size grows. In its likelihood-based form, BIC is often written as:

$$\text{BIC} = -2\,(\text{log-likelihood}) + k \log n,$$

where n is the number of observations.

Again, the key structure is:

- Better fit (higher log-likelihood) reduces the first term.
- More parameters increase the second term.
- The penalty per parameter grows with $\log n$.

How to interpret BIC in trading research.

- **Lower BIC is better.** Like AIC, the model with the lowest BIC among candidates is preferred.
- **Stronger penalty, especially with larger n.** Because the penalty term is $k \log n$, the cost of additional parameters increases with sample size. In sufficiently large samples, BIC tends to favor simpler models more strongly than AIC.
- **Approximate Bayesian flavor.** While we avoid formal Bayesian derivations here, it is useful to read BIC as: "How much posterior support does this model get from the data, if we also prefer simpler models a priori?"

When AIC and BIC disagree.

In practice, AIC and BIC often rank models similarly, but not always:

- AIC is more willing to keep slightly helpful parameters. It is better suited to prediction-focused tasks where capturing all useful signal, even weak, matters.

- BIC is more ruthless toward complexity. It is more conservative and leans toward finding the "true" underlying model in large samples.

In a trading context with relatively small and noisy samples, the difference can be meaningful:

- AIC might choose a richer specification, saying: "Given how noisy returns are, we need flexibility to exploit whatever predictive power exists."
- BIC might strip the model down, saying: "Given limited evidence and heavy penalties, the data do not justify those extra features."

As a researcher, viewing both can be illuminating. If only a very flexible model looks good by AIC and even that is not supported by BIC, you should be suspicious that you are close to, or in, the overfitting regime described earlier.

From Criteria to Coding: The Minimum Description Length View

AIC and BIC are framed in terms of likelihoods and penalties, which may feel abstract or model-specific. MDL offers a unifying and intuitive perspective: *the best model is the one that compresses the data the most.*

MDL in plain language

Imagine that you want to send the historical return series of a strategy to a colleague using as few bits as possible. You are allowed two steps:

- **Send the model.** You specify the functional form (e.g., a regression with certain predictors) and the parameter values.
- **Send the residual surprises.** After your colleague applies the model to reconstruct predicted returns, you send the remaining differences (residuals).

The total message length is:

Total description length = (bits to describe the model) + (bits to describe the residuals).

- A very simple model (few parameters, rigid structure) is cheap to describe, but its residuals may be large and unpredictable, requiring many bits to encode.
- A very complex model (many parameters, flexible structure) is expensive to describe, but can make residuals smaller and more regular, requiring fewer bits.

MDL says: choose the model that minimizes the *total* number of bits. In that sense, MDL explicitly encodes the trade-off between underfitting (short model, long residuals) and overfitting (long model, short residuals).

How this maps to AIC and BIC

Without going into derivations, you can think of AIC and BIC as particular approximations to this MDL idea:

- The negative log-likelihood is directly related to how many bits are needed to encode the residuals.
- The penalty term in AIC or BIC roughly corresponds to how many bits are needed to encode the model parameters.

Thus, when you minimize AIC or BIC, you are in effect minimizing an approximate description length. This makes MDL a useful conceptual umbrella:

> Each new trading rule, breakpoint, or filter is "paid for" by additional description length. It must reduce the complexity of the residuals enough to justify its own descriptive cost.

Trading Interpretation: Honest Description vs. Storytelling

Translating MDL into trading research language, we can make the following associations:

- **Bits to describe the model.** These correspond to:
  - Number of parameters (lookbacks, thresholds, weights).
  - Number and complexity of transformations (volatility scaling, winsorization, non-linear mappings).
  - Number of structural choices (regime definitions, breakpoints, filters).

  Every such choice must be communicated to a future implementer. The more special cases and exceptions, the longer the description.

- **Bits to describe the residuals.** These relate to:
  - How unexpected the sequence of realized returns is after conditioning on the model.
  - In practice, this boils down to how well the model captures the systematic, predictable part of returns.

  A model that explains more of the heat and cold of returns makes the residual pattern more regular and easier to "compress".

Under this view, an overfitted backtest is akin to an elaborate bedtime story: lots of details, exceptions, and special-case filters that jointly retell the history almost verbatim. The description is long, but very specific to the path you have already seen. Its true explanatory power—its ability to summarize the underlying mechanism that will persist—is weak.

An MDL mindset pushes back against such storytelling. When you find yourself adding rules like:

- "Skip trades on Mondays after FOMC weeks unless VIX is below its 20-day median,"

- "Use a different smoothing parameter in 2010–2012 because of the European crisis,"

you should mentally tally the bits you are spending. Unless these additions produce *large* and *robust* improvements in fit across samples, they are simply inflating your model description without earning their keep.

Simple Illustrative Example: Two Similar Sharpes, Different Stories

Consider two candidate strategies tested on the same daily data set:

- **Strategy A (simple).** One signal (12-month momentum), one lookback parameter, no filters. Equal-weighted portfolio, monthly rebalancing. Estimated Sharpe: 0.9.
- **Strategy B (complex).** Three signals (12-month momentum, short-term reversal, volume-based indicator); each has its own parameter; plus a volatility filter and a market-regime filter. Nonlinear combination of signals. Estimated Sharpe: 1.0.

Naively, you might prefer Strategy B: higher Sharpe and more sophistication. But suppose you compute AIC and BIC for both (using a suitable likelihood for return innovations) and obtain:

- Strategy A: lower AIC and lower BIC.
- Strategy B: slightly higher log-likelihood, but much larger penalties due to extra parameters and filters; overall higher (worse) AIC and BIC.

From the information criteria perspective, Strategy A is preferable. Its description is shorter and, once penalties are factored in, its slightly worse fit is more than compensated by its parsimony. In MDL terms, Strategy A compresses the data more efficiently: fewer bits for the model, slightly more for residuals, but less in total.

This is exactly the kind of ranking reversal we should *welcome*. It tempers our natural attraction to more elaborate stories and reminds us that a higher in-sample Sharpe can be a mirage when obtained at the cost of substantial hidden complexity.

Using Information Criteria in Day-to-Day Research

How should a practitioner incorporate AIC, BIC, and MDL into a trading research workflow? A few practical guidelines:

- **Use AIC/BIC to compare nested and nearby models.** When you are debating:
  - Whether to add another predictor,
  - Whether to introduce a breakpoint or regime,
  - Whether to use a more flexible functional form,

  compute AIC and BIC for the alternatives. If the more complex model does not produce a *meaningful* reduction in both criteria, favor the simpler version.

- **Be explicit about what counts as a parameter.** In your implementation, treat:
  - Data filters,
  - Hand-crafted event exclusions,
  - Manually tuned thresholds and breakpoints,

  as contributing to model complexity, even if they are not explicit numeric parameters in a statistical package. MDL is about description length, not just the count returned by a regression routine.

- **Track cumulative complexity over time.** As a strategy evolves, maintain a log of:
  - New signals or features added,
  - New filters or special cases introduced,

  - Changes in portfolio construction rules.

  If the AIC/BIC-like penalty you would assign to these additions grows steadily while performance does not improve commensurately, you are likely facing "model creep" and increasing overfit risk.

- **Use MDL as a mindset, not just a formula.** Even when formal likelihoods are hard to define (for example, with highly non-standard or path-dependent strategies), you can still adopt MDL's core question: "Could I describe this strategy and its performance behavior concisely to another quant who has not seen the data?" If the honest answer is "only with several pages of rules and caveats," your model is probably too complex for the available evidence.

- **Combine with out-of-sample validation.** Information criteria and MDL are not substitutes for held-out testing or cross-validation; they are complements. A model that both:

  - Scores well on AIC/BIC relative to alternatives, and
  - Holds up in out-of-sample or forward performance,

  enjoys much stronger support than one that only passes either criterion in isolation.

From Shortest Description to Robust Performance

Information criteria and MDL bring us back to a central theme of this chapter: in a world of short, noisy financial samples, we should distrust complexity unless it is overwhelmingly justified. These tools formalize that distrust. By reframing model selection as a search for the *shortest convincing explanation*, they counterbalance our temptation to chase in-sample Sharpe.

In the next sections, we will apply similar thinking directly to performance metrics themselves. We will see how raw Sharpe ratios can be adjusted for sampling error, non-normality, and—crucially—the sheer number of models we have tried, enabling us to translate the excitement of a backtest into more realistic confidence levels.

4.3 Sharpe Ratio Adjustments: PSR and DSR

In the previous sections we built two pieces of intuition. First, complex models sitting on the wrong side of the bias–variance curve systematically overfit short, noisy financial samples. Second, information criteria and Minimum Description Length help us penalize models that tell needlessly complicated stories about the data. In this section we bring those insights directly to the performance metric quants use most: the Sharpe ratio.

Our aim is twofold:

- Explain why raw Sharpe ratios routinely overstate true performance, especially in realistic trading settings with non-normal returns and heavy model mining.
- Introduce two tools—the Probabilistic Sharpe Ratio (PSR) and the Deflated Sharpe Ratio (DSR)—that convert a backtest Sharpe into a more honest measure of confidence.

Why the Raw Sharpe Is Optimistic

The annualized Sharpe ratio is typically computed as

$$\widehat{S} = \frac{\widehat{\mu}}{\widehat{\sigma}},$$

where $\widehat{\mu}$ is an estimate of the strategy's expected excess return and $\widehat{\sigma}$ is an estimate of its volatility. In theory, if returns were independent, identically distributed, and roughly normal, this simple statistic would be a decent summary of risk-adjusted performance.

In trading practice, three issues make the raw Sharpe overly optimistic.

1. Finite-sample noise and estimation error

Any Sharpe you compute is based on a finite sample. Even if the true Sharpe were, say, 0.5, your estimate will fluctuate due to randomness in returns:

- With a long sample and strong signal, the estimate will cluster near the truth.
- With a short sample or weak signal, the estimate will be very noisy.

This estimation error alone can easily move an observed Sharpe from 0.5 to 1.0 or back again. The shorter the backtest and the lower the true edge, the more "wiggle room" noise has to create eye-catching Sharpe ratios.

2. Return non-normality and dependence

Real strategy returns are rarely normal or independent:

- **Fat tails and skewness.** Many strategies have rare but severe losses (negative skewness, fat left tails). The Sharpe ratio treats all volatility symmetrically and hides how much of it comes from catastrophic events.
- **Serial correlation.** Daily or weekly returns can be autocorrelated, especially for illiquid or smoothed strategies. Overlapping positions and mark-to-model valuations can artificially reduce measured volatility and inflate Sharpe.

These features distort the sampling distribution of $\widehat{S}$: confidence intervals based on simple textbook formulas become invalid, and naive interpretations ("Sharpe of 2 means superb strategy") break down.

3. Model mining and multiple comparisons

Perhaps the most insidious source of optimism is model mining. You rarely evaluate a single strategy; instead you:

- Try many parameter combinations.
- Test many signals and transformations.
- Refine filters and portfolio rules.

Each one produces its own Sharpe ratio. Even if every candidate strategy has *zero* true edge, you are almost guaranteed to observe some seemingly impressive Sharpe ratios in-sample. By selecting the highest

Sharpe ex post, you implicitly condition on a favorable noise realization.

Thus, the raw Sharpe is doubly optimistic:

- It ignores sampling uncertainty and non-normality.
- It ignores that you selected the winner after a search.

The tools in this section aim to correct, or at least quantify, these forms of optimism.

Sharpe as a Random Variable

To make progress, it helps to change perspective. Instead of treating Sharpe as a fixed attribute of the strategy, think of the *estimated* Sharpe $\widehat{S}$ as a random variable:

- It depends on the particular sample of returns you happened to observe.
- Different samples would have produced different Sharpe estimates.

From this viewpoint, what you really want to know is not "what is $\widehat{S}$?" but:

> Given the sample I have, the length of the backtest, and the distribution of returns, what can I say about the *true* Sharpe S^* that will hold going forward?

The Probabilistic Sharpe Ratio (PSR) answers this question directly by attaching a probability to the statement "S^* exceeds some benchmark." The Deflated Sharpe Ratio (DSR) then layers in the effect of searching across many strategies.

The Probabilistic Sharpe Ratio (PSR)

The Probabilistic Sharpe Ratio starts from the idea that, conditional on a finite sample, your estimated Sharpe has an uncertainty distribution.

PSR asks:

> What is the probability that the true Sharpe S^* exceeds a chosen threshold S_0, given what we have observed?

Ingredients for PSR

To compute a PSR you need:

- The sample Sharpe ratio $\widehat{S}$ from your backtest.
- The sample size n (effective number of independent return observations).
- Some information about the return distribution, typically estimates of skewness and kurtosis, to account for non-normality.

Using these, one can approximate the sampling distribution of $\widehat{S}$, even when returns are not exactly normal. The details involve moderate-statistics and adjustments for skewness and fat tails, but conceptually you are:

- Estimating how uncertain your Sharpe estimate is.
- Computing how much of that uncertainty lies above or below the benchmark S_0.

Interpreting PSR

The output of PSR is a number between 0 and 1. For example:

- A PSR of 0.95 with respect to $S_0 = 0$ means: *Given the data, there is a 95% probability that the true Sharpe is positive.*
- A PSR of 0.60 with respect to $S_0 = 1$ means: *There is only a 60% probability that the true Sharpe is at least 1.*

PSR reframes the conversation from "the backtest Sharpe is 1.4" to "we are X% confident the true Sharpe exceeds Y." That is a much healthier way to make risk and allocation decisions.

Illustrative PSR example

Suppose a daily strategy over five years (around 1,250 observations) has:

- Estimated annualized Sharpe $\widehat{S} = 1.4$.
- Returns showing mild negative skew and fat tails (common for trend-following or carry strategies).

A PSR calculation might reveal:

- PSR relative to $S_0 = 0$: 0.99 (very high confidence the true Sharpe is positive).
- PSR relative to $S_0 = 1$: 0.70 (only 70% confidence the true Sharpe exceeds 1).

The raw Sharpe of 1.4 sounding "excellent" is tempered by the recognition that, once we account for sample length and non-normality, our confidence that the true Sharpe is actually above 1 is far from absolute.

From PSR to DSR: Adjusting for Model Mining

PSR corrects for sampling noise and non-normal returns, but it still implicitly assumes that you are assessing a single pre-specified strategy. In reality, you have typically:

- Searched parameter grids.
- Tried alternative features.
- Tinkered with filters and execution rules.

Even if you never wrote them all down, these trials matter: they increase the chance that the best Sharpe among the lot is just a lucky outlier.

The Deflated Sharpe Ratio (DSR) adjusts for this by effectively asking:

> Compared with what I would expect from picking the maximum Sharpe out of many noise-only strategies, how impressive is my observed Sharpe?

Core idea of DSR

The DSR proceeds in three conceptual steps:

- **Estimate the distribution of Sharpe ratios under the null.** Assume the true Sharpe of all candidate strategies is zero (or some low baseline), and use sample size and return non-normality to approximate how their estimated Sharpes would be distributed.
- **Account for the number of trials.** If you effectively tried M different specifications, the maximum Sharpe you would expect to see under the null is not zero, but some positive value. The more you search, the higher this expected maximum.
- **Compare your observed Sharpe to this "deflated" benchmark.** Rather than measuring how far above zero your Sharpe is, you measure how far above the expected best-of-M noise strategies it lies.

The result is a transformed Sharpe ratio that:

- Shrinks as M grows (more aggressive model mining).
- Shrinks as returns become more non-normal (heavier tails increase the chance of extreme sample outcomes).

Interpreting DSR

Like PSR, DSR can be translated into a probability or confidence measure. Informally:

- A high DSR means: *Even after accounting for how many speeds and feeds I tried, this Sharpe is unlikely to be pure luck.*
- A low or near-zero DSR means: *Given my search process, this Sharpe is about what I would expect from noise.*

DSR is thus a direct diagnostic of overfitting. It quantifies how much of your apparent edge could plausibly be the result of having looked too hard at the data.

Worked Numeric Illustration

To see how PSR and DSR change our view of performance, consider three stylized strategies, each tested over the same time period:

- **Strategy 1 (modest search).** You tried 5 sensible variations and selected the best one. The chosen backtest shows a Sharpe of 0.9.
- **Strategy 2 (intensive search).** You tried about 100 variations (different lags, filters, and portfolio rules) and selected the top performer. The chosen backtest shows a Sharpe of 1.4.
- **Strategy 3 (very intensive search).** You ran a wide, exploratory search with roughly 500 variations and then cherry-picked the best-looking result. The chosen backtest shows a Sharpe of 1.8.

Assume all three use daily data over 5 years (about 1,250 observations) and have similar skewness and kurtosis characteristics. A possible set of adjusted metrics might look like the following (conceptually):

- **Strategy 1**
  - Raw Sharpe: 0.9
  - PSR vs $S_0 = 0$: 0.97
  - DSR-implied effective Sharpe: around 0.8 (minor deflation; limited search).
- **Strategy 2**
  - Raw Sharpe: 1.4
  - PSR vs $S_0 = 0$: 0.99
  - PSR vs $S_0 = 1$: 0.70
  - DSR-implied effective Sharpe: around 0.9 (substantial deflation due to 100 trials).
- **Strategy 3**
  - Raw Sharpe: 1.8

  - PSR vs $S_0 = 0$: 0.995
  - PSR vs $S_0 = 1$: 0.85
  - DSR-implied effective Sharpe: around 0.8 (heavy deflation; 500 trials mean a high expected best-of-noise Sharpe).

An important qualitative lesson emerges:

- Strategy 2 and Strategy 3, despite higher raw Sharpes, may not be more trustworthy than Strategy 1 once we account properly for noise and model mining.
- The DSR pulls the effective Sharpe of heavily-mined strategies back toward more modest levels, exposing how much of their apparent excellence may be luck.

Practical Guidelines for Using PSR and DSR

To incorporate these ideas into a trading research process, consider the following guidelines.

1. Always accompany Sharpe with uncertainty

Instead of reporting a single Sharpe number, add:

- PSR relative to a low baseline (e.g., $S_0 = 0$) to show the probability that the strategy has any edge at all.
- PSR relative to a higher benchmark (e.g., $S_0 = 1$) to communicate how confident you are that the edge is strong enough to matter operationally.

This forces you and your stakeholders to think in probabilistic terms, aligning expectations with statistical reality.

2. Be honest about the breadth of your search

DSR relies on an estimate of how many strategies or specifications you effectively tried. This number rarely equals the number of strategies in a final summary table. It also includes:

- Parameter sweeps.

- Abandoned indicators and failed filters.
- Early prototypes that "did not work" and were discarded.

Documenting and quantifying this search breadth is uncomfortable but essential. Inflating or underreporting it will lead to misleading DSR adjustments.

3. Use DSR to screen out suspiciously high Sharpes

If a strategy's raw Sharpe is very high but:

- Its DSR-effective Sharpe is modest, or
- Its DSR-based confidence that $S^* > 0$ is only slightly above 50%,

then its backtest is more likely a product of overfitting than genuine edge. Treat such strategies with skepticism, regardless of their surface-level attractiveness.

4. Combine with model complexity controls

PSR and DSR complement, rather than replace, the tools from earlier sections:

- **Information criteria / MDL** help you choose among models by penalizing complexity directly.
- **PSR and DSR** help you interpret performance metrics after you have chosen a model (or a family of models).

A robust strategy will:

- Score well on AIC/BIC or MDL relative to simpler and more complex alternatives,
- Deliver a reasonably high PSR for meaningful benchmarks, and
- Maintain a solid DSR even after honest accounting of the research search.

5. Set internal thresholds in terms of adjusted metrics

Rather than adopting rules like "we require a Sharpe of 1.5 in backtest," consider:

- Minimum PSR (e.g., "PSR relative to 0.5 must exceed 80%").
- Minimum DSR-effective Sharpe (e.g., "DSR-adjusted Sharpe must be at least 0.5").

This aligns decision-making with the true quantity of interest: reliable, out-of-sample performance, not just an inflated in-sample statistic.

From Excitement to Confidence

The raw Sharpe ratio is a compelling headline number. It compresses a lot of information into a single scalar and lends itself to easy comparisons and storytelling. Unfortunately, in the context of short, noisy, non-normal financial data and aggressive research processes, it is also a serial exaggerator.

The Probabilistic Sharpe Ratio forces you to confront the fragility of your estimates in finite samples. The Deflated Sharpe Ratio goes further by holding you accountable for the sheer number of models you have tried. Together, they translate backtest excitement into more realistic confidence levels.

In the next section, we will generalize this logic beyond a single strategy. We will ask, at the level of the entire research process: given the way we search and select models, what is the probability that our chosen winner is actually an overfit to historical noise? That is the role of the Probability of Backtest Overfitting (PBO).

4.4 Probability of Backtest Overfitting

The previous sections attacked overfitting along three fronts. We examined how excessive model complexity and aggressive parameter search push us into a high-variance regime; we saw how information criteria and MDL penalize complex stories that do not earn their keep; and we adjusted the Sharpe ratio with PSR and DSR to correct for sampling noise and model mining.

All of these tools, however, operate at the level of a *single* strategy and its immediate variations. They tell you how much confidence to place in one backtest after the fact. In practice, research groups often maintain whole libraries of candidate strategies and routinely run large batches of backtests. What we would like is a diagnostic that speaks to the entire *research process*:

> Given the way we search across many candidate specifications, what is the probability that the strategy we have chosen as "best" is an artifact of overfitting?

The Probability of Backtest Overfitting (PBO) provides exactly this: a formal, data-driven estimate of how likely it is that your in-sample winner will turn out to be a loser out-of-sample, *relative to the set of alternatives you considered.* It does so by combining cross-validation with a careful account of how often top-ranked strategies fail to hold their rank out-of-sample.

From Point Estimates to Process-Level Risk

PSR and DSR reframed the Sharpe ratio as a random variable and asked: "How likely is it that this Sharpe reflects real edge?" PBO extends the same logic, but now across a *universe* of candidate strategies. Conceptually:

- You start with M candidate strategies (different signals, parameterizations, portfolio rules, and so on).
- You have a historical sample of length T (e.g., 10 years of daily data).
- You want to know: if you pick the best backtest in-sample, how often would that chosen winner underperform a typical alternative when tested on unseen data?

PBO answers this by simulating, in a structured way, what would have happened if history had unfolded slightly differently. Instead of a single train-test split, it repeatedly reshuffles the sample into many overlapping train-test pairs and tracks how often the in-sample winner fails out-of-sample.

Basic Intuition: How Often Does the Champion Collapse?

Imagine you have a league of trading strategies. In your historical "season," each strategy plays every period (month, quarter, or year) and accumulates performance. At the end of the season, you rank them and pick the champion: the strategy with the highest in-sample Sharpe or P&L.

Now imagine that you could replay the season many times, but with slightly different schedules:

- You slice the full history into segments.
- In each experiment, you let the strategies compete in some segments (the training set) and then see how they do in the remaining segments (the test set).

In each experiment, you ask:

> Did the champion of the training set remain strong in the test set, or did it fall to the bottom of the league?

PBO formally quantifies how frequently the latter happens. A high PBO means that your process tends to elevate strategies that look great in-sample but systematically underperform out-of-sample relative to their peers.

Combinatorial Cross-Validation: The Engine Behind PBO

Standard cross-validation usually relies on a small number of train-test splits (for example, 70% of data for training, 30% for testing). PBO uses a richer approach called *combinatorial cross-validation* over contiguous time blocks. The idea is to:

1. Partition the time series into S non-overlapping, contiguous subperiods (e.g., 8 or 10 blocks of equal length).

2. Consider many different ways of designating some of these blocks as the training set and the remaining blocks as the test set, always keeping the time order intact within each block.

Each such assignment of blocks yields one cross-validation experiment:

- You estimate and rank strategies on the training blocks.
- You then evaluate the same strategies on the test blocks.

By iterating over many combinations, you get a rich empirical picture of how often in-sample winners fail out-of-sample.

Step-by-Step PBO Algorithm

Let us now describe the PBO procedure more systematically. Suppose you have:

- M candidate strategies.
- A historical sample of T periods (for example, monthly returns over 15 years).
- A choice of S contiguous subperiods (for example, $S = 8$ blocks of roughly equal length).

The PBO algorithm proceeds as follows.

1. Partition the data into subperiods

Break the time series into S contiguous blocks:

$$\text{Block } 1, \text{ Block } 2, \ldots, \text{ Block } S.$$

These might be, for instance, rolling three-year windows, calendar years, or equal-length intervals. The key is that:

- Each block is used as a whole; we do not shuffle individual observations.

- This respects time ordering and allows each block to represent a plausible market regime.

2. Enumerate train-test combinations

Choose a rule for splitting blocks into training and test sets. A common choice is:

- For each experiment, select half of the blocks as training and use the remaining half as test.

You then consider many such combinations (in principle, all combinations of size $S/2$ from S, but in practice, you may subsample if S is large). Each combination defines:

- A training sample (concatenation of the chosen blocks in chronological order).
- A test sample (concatenation of the remaining blocks in chronological order).

3. Train and rank strategies in-sample

For a given train-test split:

1. Compute a performance metric (e.g., Sharpe ratio) for each of the M strategies using only the training sample.
2. Rank the strategies from best to worst according to this in-sample metric.
3. Identify the in-sample champion: the strategy with the highest training performance.

4. Evaluate the champion out-of-sample

Using the same train-test split:

1. Compute the performance metric for *all* M strategies on the test sample.

2. Find the rank of the in-sample champion *within the test sample.* This yields an out-of-sample performance rank for the previously selected winner.

To make ranks comparable across experiments, we often convert them into a relative position between 0 and 1. For example:

- Rank 1 out of M maps to a high quantile close to 1.
- Rank M (worst) maps to a quantile near 0.

5. Repeat across many splits

Repeat steps 2–4 across many different train-test block combinations. For each experiment, you record:

- The in-sample champion.
- Its out-of-sample performance rank (or quantile) among all strategies.

Over many runs, you build a distribution of out-of-sample quantiles for in-sample champions.

6. Compute PBO

The Probability of Backtest Overfitting is then defined as:

> PBO = fraction of experiments in which the in-sample champion's out-of-sample rank falls *below* the median (or some chosen threshold) among all strategies.

Equivalently, you can say:

- If PBO = 0.7, then in about 70% of the cross-validation experiments, the in-sample champion performs worse than a typical strategy out-of-sample.
- If PBO = 0.2, then in only 20% of experiments does the champion fall below the median out-of-sample rank; the process appears less prone to overfitting.

A high PBO indicates that your research and selection process is systematically picking noise-fitting strategies that do not generalize well. A low PBO suggests that your in-sample ranking carries real information about future relative performance.

Flow Diagram of the PBO Procedure

The following schematic summarizes the steps just described, highlighting how data flows from partitioning through training, testing, and aggregation into a PBO estimate.

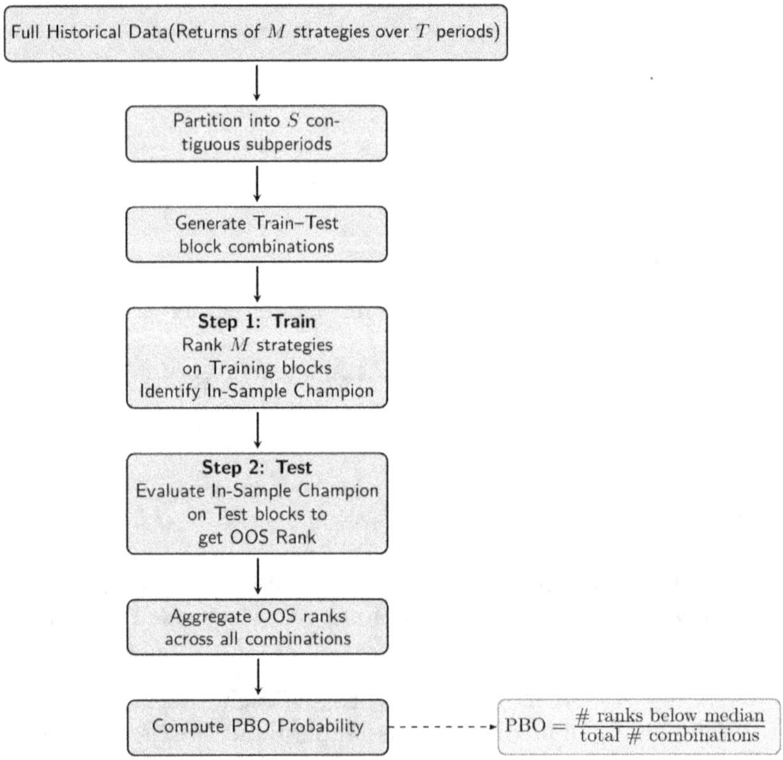

Interpreting PBO in Practice

PBO turns an abstract concern—"we may be overfitting"—into a quantitative risk measure between 0 and 1. Some practical interpretations:

- **PBO close to 0.5 or higher.** Your selection process is barely better than random in terms of out-of-sample rankings; in extreme cases (PBO $\approx$ 0.7 or 0.8), the champion is more often a future underperformer than not. This is a strong indication of heavy overfitting.
- **PBO well below 0.5.** In-sample winners tend to remain competitive out-of-sample. This does not guarantee profitability, but it suggests that your ranking carries genuine predictive information.
- **PBO near 0.** In-sample champions almost always remain near the top out-of-sample. This is rare in finance and usually indicates either:

- A very strong and stable underlying effect, or
- A flawed validation design (for example, leakage between training and test sets).

How PBO Relates to PSR and DSR

It is helpful to view PBO, PSR, and DSR as complementary layers:

- **PSR** focuses on a single strategy's Sharpe and asks: "Given sample size and non-normality, how likely is it that the true Sharpe exceeds threshold S_0?"
- **DSR** modifies that answer by accounting for how many strategies you effectively searched over before choosing this one.
- **PBO** steps back and evaluates the entire selection mechanism across many splits, asking: "How often does the in-sample champion end up below average out-of-sample?"

Where DSR uses analytic approximations rooted in distributional assumptions, PBO is more empirical and simulation-driven. It does not directly correct a Sharpe ratio; instead, it tells you about the *reliability* of the process that produced that Sharpe.

Stylized Example: Rising PBO with Search Intensity

Consider three research setups, each with the same pool of potential signals but different degrees of restraint:

- Setup A (disciplined). You pre-specify 10 plausible strategies based on strong economic reasoning and limited parameter variation. You run PBO with $M = 10$.
- Setup B (moderate mining). You allow 100 strategies, including broader parameter sweeps and extra filters, but still within a coherent theme.
- Setup C (aggressive mining). You explore 500+ strategies, including many loosely motivated combinations and exotic transformations.

Running the PBO algorithm on each setup over the same historical period might yield results like:

- Setup A: PBO ≈ 0.25.
- Setup B: PBO ≈ 0.45.
- Setup C: PBO ≈ 0.70.

Even if each setup produces an in-sample champion with similar raw Sharpe, their PBO values carry very different messages:

- In Setup A, there is a reasonable chance that the champion reflects a real pattern that generalizes.
- In Setup B, selection risk is already large: in almost half the cross-validation splits, the champion is below median out-of-sample.

- In Setup C, the process is dominated by overfitting: the champion is more likely to underperform than not.

This illustrates a powerful aspect of PBO: it penalizes not only individual model complexity but also the *breadth* of the strategy search itself, in a way that is grounded in actual out-of-sample behavior across many partitions.

Design Choices and Pitfalls

Like any diagnostic, PBO depends on how you set it up. Some practical considerations:

Choice of subperiods

- Blocks should be long enough to provide meaningful performance estimates (for example, at least 1–2 years of monthly data, or a few hundred intraday observations).
- Blocks should capture different regimes when possible (bull vs. bear markets, high vs. low volatility), so that cross-validation probes regime sensitivity.

Number of strategies M

- M should reflect the strategies that were actually available for selection at the time, not just the few survivors.
- Omitting unpromising candidates biases PBO downward (makes the process look safer than it is).

Choice of performance metric

- Sharpe ratio is common, but you could use other summary statistics (e.g., average return, drawdown-adjusted measures).
- The metric should be the same one you would actually use to pick a winner in real life; otherwise, PBO may not reflect your true selection behavior.

Data leakage and look-ahead

- PBO assumes that training and test blocks are separated in time and that no information leaks from test to training.
- If your implementation inadvertently reuses information from the test side (for example, by normalizing across the full sample), PBO will underestimate overfitting risk.

Using PBO as a Governance Tool

Beyond its technical definition, PBO is valuable as a governance metric inside a research organization. Some uses include:

- **Setting thresholds for deployment.** You might adopt a policy such as: "We will not deploy a new strategy if its PBO exceeds 40%, regardless of its backtest Sharpe."
- **Comparing research processes.** If one team's pipeline yields PBO values consistently around 0.3 while another's hover around 0.7, the latter process likely needs more discipline in model specification and validation.
- **Monitoring drift over time.** As your platform evolves and more features and signals are added, PBO can warn you when the increasing search space has silently raised overfitting risk, even if headline performance metrics look stable.

In these roles, PBO shifts the focus from "How good does this backtest look?" to "How trustworthy is our way of generating good-looking backtests?" That is a crucial distinction in environments where competitive pressure constantly pushes researchers toward the overfitting frontier.

From Single Backtests to Process-Level Reliability

Taken together, the tools in this chapter form a hierarchy of defenses:

- **Bias–variance mechanics and model complexity** warn us against excessively flexible models in short, noisy samples.
- **Information criteria and MDL** penalize unnecessarily long and intricate descriptions of trading behavior.
- **PSR and DSR** deflate optimistic Sharpe ratios for sampling noise and multiple testing.
- **PBO** finally audits the entire selection process, quantifying how often our champions are merely lucky noise fits.

Probabilistic measures like PSR, DSR, and PBO do not make uncertainty disappear. Instead, they describe it honestly and force us to confront the fact that pleasing backtests are cheap to manufacture. By integrating PBO into your research workflow, you move from a culture of chasing high Sharpe ratios to one of managing the probability that your models will fail exactly when you need them most: out-of-sample, in real time, with real capital at risk.

Chapter 5

Signal Decay, Regimes, and Implementation Frictions

Most quant strategies don't die in a backtest-they die in the wild. This chapter follows a signal from birth to burial, showing how decay, regime shifts, portfolio plumbing, and trading frictions quietly compress a beautiful simulated Sharpe into something barely worth deploying-and what you can do, concretely, to slow that erosion and size your bets realistically.

5.1 Concept Drift and Alpha Half-Life

In earlier chapters we treated a signal as if it were generated by a stable data-generating process: we estimated its performance on the past, applied some regularization and validation, and then projected that performance into the future. In live trading, this stability assumption is almost always false. Markets learn, institutions adapt, regulations change, and microstructure evolves. Even genuinely predictive signals have a finite shelf life.

This section introduces *signal decay* as a central concept for understanding why models that look healthy in backtests gradually turn into noise in production. We define *alpha half-life* as a practical way to summarize how quickly a signal's edge decays, and we show how to approximate it from historical data using decay curves, lagged information coefficients (IC), and rolling diagnostics. Finally, we connect half-life to *concept drift*—the change of the underlying relationship between predictors and returns—and outline a monitoring workflow that helps you detect decay before it becomes a costly surprise.

What Is Signal Decay?

A predictive signal is a mapping from observable features (prices, fundamentals, flows, text scores, and so on) to expected returns. *Signal decay* is the erosion of the predictive relationship between the signal and realized returns as time passes.

There are two complementary ways to think about this erosion:

- **Time-lag decay:** A given signal snapshot today becomes less relevant as we move further away in time. For example, a short-term mean-reversion score may be highly predictive of tomorrow's return, somewhat predictive for the next three days, and essentially useless after a week.

- **Calendar-time decay:** The same modeling recipe (features, transformations, estimation method) becomes less predictive as the market regime changes. A value factor defined in 2005 may work well in the following decade, then weaken or even reverse in 2020–2023 as the macro and competitive environment shifts.

Most quants encounter the first type when they look at how performance changes with holding period; they experience the second when a beloved strategy quietly stops working in real time. Concept drift is mainly about this second type, but to reason about it we first need to formalize the notion of time-lag decay.

Alpha Half-Life and Decay Curves

The term *alpha half-life* borrows intuition from radioactive decay. Imagine that the predictive power of a given signal "decays" smoothly as its information becomes stale. The alpha half-life is the time it takes for the signal's predictive strength to fall to half its initial level.

In practice, you approximate this using a *decay curve*: measure the signal's predictive power at different lags between signal observation and realized return. A simple version proceeds as follows for a single signal:

1. Choose a set of lags or holding horizons: for example, 1, 2, 5, 10, 20 trading days.

2. For each lag L, compute a performance metric that captures predictive power: common choices include cross-sectional IC (rank correlation between signal and future returns), t-statistics of returns from a long-short portfolio formed on the signal, or contribution to portfolio P&L.

3. Plot the metric against L to obtain a decay curve. The curve typically slopes downward: the further you look, the less of today's signal is still informative.

4. Identify the lag where the performance metric has fallen to about half its value at the shortest lag. That lag is your empirical alpha half-life.

This is not about fitting an exact functional form (exponential vs. power-law) but about getting an order-of-magnitude feel. If your signal's IC drops from 0.08 at 1 day to 0.04 at 3 days and then to 0.02 at 10 days, you can say its half-life is roughly 3 days. If instead it drops from 0.08 at 1 month to 0.04 at 6 months, you have a longer-horizon signal whose edge persists over quarters.

Right after you have this conceptual picture in mind, it is helpful to visualize it.

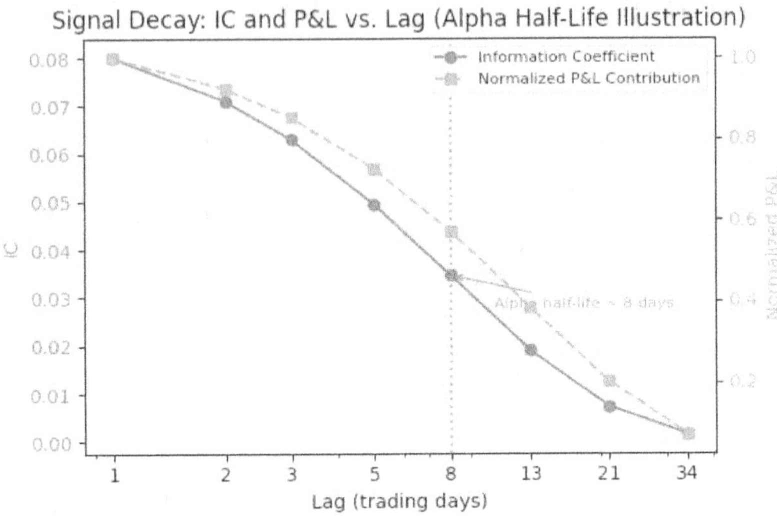

In this illustration, both IC and normalized P&L contribution decline with the lag between when the signal is observed and when returns are realized. The vertical line marks the approximate half-life, where IC has fallen to about half of its initial value at the shortest horizon.

From Lagged IC Profiles to Concept Drift

So far we have treated the underlying relationship between signal and returns as fixed and only varied the *holding period.* To talk about concept drift, we keep the holding period fixed and let the *calendar time* move.

Two simple tools are particularly useful:

- **Lagged IC profile:** At each lag (1 day, 2 days, 5 days, and so on), compute the signal's IC over a rolling window in calendar time. This lets you see whether the half-life itself is changing. A short-term signal whose 1-day IC was 0.06 in 2015–2018 but is 0.01 in 2021–2024 is a textbook example of concept drift.
- **Rolling P&L contribution:** For a portfolio that uses multi-

ple signals, attribute P&L to each signal (for example, via regression of returns on signal-implied weights) in rolling windows. A shrinking contribution, especially if it trends toward zero or changes sign, is another sign that the underlying concept is drifting.

The key mental move is to stop asking "does the signal work?" and instead ask "*when* does it work, and how fast does it degrade?" This temporal view is what connects decay curves to model monitoring.

Benign Instability vs. Concept Drift

Financial time series are inherently noisy. Metrics like IC, Sharpe ratio, and regression coefficients will bounce around simply due to randomness. You do not want to rebuild or kill a strategy every time a rolling window t-stat dips.

It is therefore useful to distinguish:

- **Benign parameter instability:** Small, reversible fluctuations in estimated parameters or performance metrics that are consistent with sampling noise. For example, an IC series that oscillates between 0.03 and 0.07 with no clear trend is often benign.
- **Concept drift:** Persistent, structural changes in the signal-return relationship that cannot realistically be attributed to noise. Examples include a long-term downward trend in IC, a shift from positive to near-zero or negative correlation, or a permanent change in volatility or cross-sectional dispersion that undermines the signal's mechanism.

Practically, you look for three patterns:

1. **Level shift:** The average IC used to be around 0.06 for several years and is now clustered around 0.01 for the last several years. That kind of sustained shift is unlikely to be pure noise.
2. **Trend:** The rolling Sharpe of the signal's standalone long-short portfolio drifts down over many windows, even though volatility and other external conditions are not dramatically changing.

3. **Shape change in the decay curve:** The whole lag profile flattens. For example, in early years the IC decays smoothly from 0.08 at 1 day to 0.03 at 5 days; in recent years the 1-day IC itself is already at 0.02 and decays almost immediately to zero. The concept has not just weakened; its effective horizon has shortened or disappeared.

Benign instability is like background chatter around a stable mean; concept drift is like the mean itself moving.

Rolling Window Backtests and Stability Plots

To separate noise from drift, you need to analyze your signal with *rolling* or *expanding* windows rather than as a single full-sample block.

A basic workflow looks like this:

1. Define the evaluation horizon.

Pick the signal horizon you care about operationally: one day, five days, one month. For that horizon, you will compute performance and diagnostics in rolling windows of calendar time.

2. Choose a window length and step.

There is a trade-off between stability and responsiveness:

- Short windows (e.g., 3–6 months for daily signals) respond quickly to changes but produce noisy statistics.
- Longer windows (e.g., 2–3 years) give more stable estimates but may hide rapid decay.

Many practitioners use overlapping windows (for example, 12-month windows that roll forward monthly) to get smoother time series without giving up timeliness entirely.

3. Compute rolling metrics.

For each window, compute:

- Cross-sectional IC for your target horizon.

- Realized Sharpe ratio of a hypothetical long-short portfolio built on the signal alone (e.g., long top decile, short bottom decile).
- Average turnover and transaction cost estimates, to see whether implementation is changing.
- Key regression coefficients if the signal is combined with others (e.g., coefficient and t-stat when regressing portfolio returns on the signal's forecast).

Plot these over time as "stability plots." A flat band around a constant level suggests stable performance; downward drifts, breaks, or volatility explosions suggest regime changes or decay.

4. Use rolling lagged IC profiles.

For each window, you can also compute the decay curve itself: IC at 1 day, 2 days, 5 days, etc. Then you either:

- Summarize each curve with a single number, such as its estimated half-life, and plot the half-life over time; or
- Visualize a small set of windows (e.g., early sample vs. late sample) on the same chart to see how the curve shape has evolved.

If you see the half-life systematically shrinking—say, from about 5 days in earlier windows to about 1–2 days more recently—you are likely witnessing concept drift.

Stress Tests for Shrinking Edge

Rolling diagnostics show you what has actually happened in historical data. To understand how fragile your edge might be going forward, you also want to perform stress tests that answer "what if" questions.

Useful stress tests include:

- **Weaker signal strength:** Halve the IC or shrink signal scores toward zero and recompute performance. This mimics a shorter half-life or partial degradation. If the strategy collapses under a modest reduction, you are highly exposed to decay.

- **Delayed execution:** Shift the assumed trading time by one or more bars (e.g., trade at the next open instead of the same close) and recompute P&L. Shorter-horizon signals whose half-life is just a day or two are particularly vulnerable: a small implementation delay can consume most of the remaining edge.
- **Reduced cross-sectional dispersion:** Many cross-sectional strategies rely on spreads between top and bottom ranked names. Simulate what happens if dispersion in signal scores narrows (for example, by compressing scores toward the mean). This can represent crowding as more capital chases the same idea, or structural shifts that reduce the spread in fundamentals.
- **Regime-specific performance:** Slice the backtest into major historical regimes (pre-crisis, crisis, post-crisis, low-rate, high-rate) and rerun the strategy in each. Signals that only work in a single regime are especially at risk once that environment changes.

These stress tests do not predict the exact path of decay, but they help quantify how much degradation your strategy can tolerate before becoming unviable.

Monitoring Rules and Intervention Triggers

Once you appreciate that all signals decay, it is natural to build monitoring into your production process. Rather than reacting ad hoc to drawdowns, you define rules that watch for patterns consistent with concept drift and then trigger appropriate interventions.

A simple, practical monitoring framework uses three layers:

1. Health indicators.

On a regular schedule (daily, weekly, or monthly, depending on horizon), compute:

- **Recent IC** over a short window (e.g., 3 months for daily signals), compared with its historical distribution.
- **Recent standalone Sharpe** of the signal's long-short test portfolio.

- **Recent P&L attribution** for strategies that combine signals.

Standardize these metrics, for example, by expressing them as z-scores relative to history. This gives a simple gauge of whether the current environment is unusually bad (or good) for the signal.

2. Thresholds and traffic lights.

Define thresholds that correspond to concern levels, such as:

- "Yellow": The rolling IC is below its long-run median for three consecutive windows, or its z-score is below -1. This may lead you to temporarily reduce risk allocated to the signal and investigate qualitatively what has changed.
- "Red": The rolling IC is near zero or negative for a sustained period (for example, one year), or the signal's P&L contribution is consistently negative after costs. This triggers a formal review, including re-estimation, feature engineering, or even decommissioning the signal.

The exact definitions depend on your risk tolerance and horizon, but the principle is to codify your response to decay rather than rely on gut feeling.

3. Feedback loops into model design.

When monitoring detects potential drift, you want to learn from it rather than just switch the strategy off. Common responses include:

- **Re-estimation:** Retrain the model with more recent data or rolling windows that overweight the last few years.
- **Feature updates:** Add or modify features to capture new drivers of returns. For instance, if liquidity conditions have changed, include liquidity proxies explicitly.
- **Horizon adjustment:** If decay curves show that the half-life has shortened, shift the strategy's target holding period or execution assumptions to align with the new reality.

- **Capacity reduction:** If crowding is a plausible cause of decay, reduce the capital deployed or spread it across more diverse instruments.

You should think of a signal not as a static object but as a living hypothesis about the market. Monitoring and intervention are the scientific method applied to that hypothesis over time.

Putting It All Together

Signal decay and concept drift are not edge cases; they are the default. Every backtest you run is implicitly a snapshot of a relationship that may already be fading. Alpha half-life gives you a simple summary of how quickly a given signal's information becomes stale in time. Decay curves and lagged IC profiles extend this into a richer picture of both time-lag and calendar-time decay.

By embedding rolling diagnostics, stability plots, and stress tests into your workflow, you move from a static view of "this signal works" to a dynamic view of "this is how long it tends to work, and this is how we will know when it is failing." The next sections will build on this idea by formalizing regime detection and change-point methods, which give you more structured tools to understand when the environment itself has shifted so far that yesterday's alpha has become today's noise.

5.2 Regime Detection and Change-Point Methods

In the previous section we treated decay mainly as a gradual process: a signal's information content fades, its alpha half-life shrinks, and its diagnostics drift over time. That picture already warned us that a single full-sample backtest can hide important temporal variation in performance.

Real markets, however, often change not just gradually but in *lumps*. Policy regimes flip, liquidity conditions jump, correlations reorganize in crises, new participants enter or exit. These *regime shifts* and *struc-*

tural breaks can turn a historically robust signal into a dead trade almost overnight, or, more subtly, make a multi-year backtest look stable even though the strategy only works in one type of environment.

This section develops tools to make your validation *state-aware*. We will:

- Clarify what we mean by regimes and structural breaks.
- Show how pooling across regimes can distort Sharpe ratios and other statistics.
- Introduce practical diagnostics for detecting breaks and shifts.
- Outline simple regime-labelling approaches—from handcrafted rules to clustering and hidden Markov models—that you can layer onto your backtests.
- Show how to use these labels to evaluate whether a signal truly survives across regimes or is just a "single-regime trade wearing a multi-year backtest disguise."

What Are Regimes and Structural Breaks?

A *regime* is a period during which the key statistical properties of the market relevant to your strategy are roughly stable. Examples include:

- Low-volatility, low-rate environments with ample liquidity and tight spreads.
- Crisis episodes with elevated volatility, wide spreads, and stronger cross-asset correlations.
- Trend-dominated markets where momentum strategies thrive.
- Oscillatory or range-bound markets where mean-reversion dominates.

A *structural break* is a point in time where those properties change in a lasting way. For example:

- A major monetary policy shift (e.g., zero-rate policy to a rapid hiking cycle).
- A regulatory change that bans a popular trading practice or alters leverage.
- The introduction of a new trading venue or technology that affects microstructure.
- A crisis or crash that permanently changes risk appetite and correlation structures.

In statistical terms, a structural break is a change in the parameters or distribution of the process generating returns, volatility, correlations, or other variables your strategy depends on.

Level Shifts vs. Volatility Shifts

Not all breaks are the same. Two types are especially important for strategy evaluation:

Level shifts: The mean of a process changes, but its variability does not. For example, the expected equity risk premium might step up or down; a carry trade's average return might drop after a regulatory change, even if its volatility is unchanged.

Volatility shifts: The variability increases or decreases while the mean might stay similar. For example, a long/short equity book may see similar average returns but much higher volatility during crisis regimes.

Why does this distinction matter? Because pooled statistics can mask the underlying story:

- Pooling a high-mean, low-vol regime with a low-mean, high-vol regime can produce a deceptive "average" Sharpe ratio that you never actually experience in either regime.
- A strategy that is only profitable in a low-vol regime may still show an attractive full-sample Sharpe if that regime dominates the historical period, even if the same strategy performs poorly or catastrophically in crises.

Your goal is not just to know that a strategy has a Sharpe of, say, 1.2 over twenty years, but to understand *how that Sharpe is assembled* from very different environments.

How Regime Pooling Distorts Backtests

To see how pooling can mislead, imagine a simple long/short equity strategy:

- In Calm Regimes (80% of the backtest), the strategy earns +12% per year with 10% volatility: Sharpe around 1.2.
- In Crisis Regimes (20% of the backtest), it loses -15% per year with 25% volatility: Sharpe around -0.6.

If you pool the entire period, you might see something like +7% average return with 13% volatility, which corresponds to a Sharpe roughly around 0.5. That number is technically correct but strategically incomplete:

- It suggests a moderate edge but hides the fact the strategy is *strongly regime-dependent.*
- It does not reveal that most of the positive P&L comes from one type of environment, and that the strategy is actively harmful in another.
- It gives you no guidance on what to expect if the future looks more like the crisis regime than the calm one.

Regime-aware analysis instead asks:

> In which regimes does the signal earn money? In which does it lose? What is the probability and duration of those regimes? How painful is it to hold the strategy through unfavourable ones?

To answer these questions, you need to segment your sample into regimes and then evaluate performance conditional on those regimes.

Simple Rolling Diagnostics for Regime Suspicion

Before you deploy more formal methods, you can often detect regime changes with simple rolling statistics on returns and risk.

Rolling mean and variance.

Pick a window length that balances noise and responsiveness (for example, 3–6 months for daily data, 1–2 years for monthly data), then compute:

- Rolling mean return of the strategy or factor portfolio.
- Rolling volatility (standard deviation) over the same window.

Plot these time series together with vertical lines marking major economic or market events. Sudden and persistent shifts in the rolling mean or variance are a first hint that you may have moved into a new regime.

Rolling cross-asset correlations.

Many strategies rely on assumptions about cross-asset relationships: diversification across sectors, low correlation between asset classes, stable factor loadings, and so on. Compute rolling correlations such as:

- Correlation between your strategy and major risk factors (market, value, momentum, carry).
- Average pairwise correlation among the assets in your universe.
- Correlation between key macro variables and your returns.

When these correlations jump and stay at new levels, it suggests a change in the underlying network of relationships—a regime shift in correlation structure.

Rolling distributional diagnostics.

You can also monitor:

- Rolling skewness and kurtosis of returns to detect tail behaviour changes.

- Frequency and magnitude of drawdowns over time.

A period with frequent large drawdowns and fat tails is qualitatively a different regime from one with small, normally-distributed fluctuations, even if average returns are similar.

These rolling diagnostics do not formally locate change-points, but they tell you where to look more closely.

Change-Point Detection: Locating Structural Breaks

Change-point methods attempt to algorithmically identify times at which the statistical properties of a series change. Think of them as tools that propose candidate regime boundaries for further inspection.

CUSUM-Based Tests

One of the simplest and most widely used classes of methods is based on cumulative sums of deviations, often abbreviated as CUSUM.

The intuition is straightforward:

- Suppose returns have a stable mean. If you accumulate deviations from that mean, the cumulative sum should oscillate around zero.
- If the mean shifts up or down at some point, the cumulative sum starts drifting consistently upward or downward from that point.

A CUSUM procedure:

- Computes cumulative sums of standardized deviations from a reference level (e.g., pre-sample mean).
- Monitors whether those cumulative sums cross certain thresholds.
- Flags a change-point when the thresholds are breached.

In practice, you can apply CUSUM to:

- Strategy returns, to detect shifts in mean performance.
- Squared returns, to detect volatility shifts.
- Risk factor exposures or regression residuals, to detect when the relationship between signal and returns has changed.

CUSUM is attractive because it is simple and fast; however, it will trigger both on transient shocks and on persistent changes. You therefore use it as a starting point and then cross-check flagged dates against economic intuition and other diagnostics.

Offline vs. Online Change-Point Detection

You can apply change-point methods in two ways:

Offline (retrospective): Given a full historical series, find one or more points that best explain the data as a sequence of segments with different parameters. This is what you usually do in research to understand historical regimes: for example, split a 20-year backtest into three segments that differ in mean and variance.

Online (sequential): As new data arrives, update statistics and ask whether the most recent observations are likely to come from the same regime as the past. This is closer to what you want in live monitoring: detect early if the environment for your strategy has changed.

Some algorithms explicitly target multiple change-points (e.g., dynamic programming methods that partition the series into many segments while penalizing over-segmentation), while others enforce at most one break. In practice, it is usually more useful to identify a small number of economically interpretable breaks than to chase every micro-change.

Other Change-Point Tools

Beyond CUSUM, there is a broad toolbox:

- **Likelihood-based methods:** Fit parametric models (e.g., normal with different means/variances) on candidate segments and choose breakpoints that maximise overall likelihood with penalties for complexity.
- **Nonparametric methods:** Use statistics based on ranks or

distribution distances to detect changes without assuming a specific distribution.

- **Multivariate methods:** Extend the idea to multiple series jointly (returns, volatility proxies, correlations) to find breaks in the joint behaviour.

For most practical trading research, you do not need exotic methods. A combination of rolling diagnostics, basic CUSUM or likelihood tests, and economic reasoning often suffices to identify a reasonable set of candidate regime boundaries.

Regime Labelling: Turning Breaks into States

Change-points give you candidate boundaries; *regime labelling* assigns a state or label to each period. The label is a short description of the environment: "low-vol carry regime," "crisis regime," "post-crisis recovery," and so on. Once you have labels, you can condition all your validation metrics on them.

Regime labelling can be done at several levels of sophistication.

Rule-Based Regime Definitions

The simplest approach is to define regimes by hand using observable quantities:

- **Volatility buckets:** Label periods as "low-vol" when index volatility is below a threshold; "medium-vol" for intermediate ranges; "high-vol" when above a higher threshold.

- **Trend vs. range-bound:** Compute a trend indicator (e.g., moving-average crossover) on a benchmark index. Label days with strong trend signals as "trending" and others as "range." Evaluate your momentum or mean-reversion signal in each.

- **Policy or macro regimes:** Use known dates of policy shifts (e.g., pre-/post-introduction of a monetary policy framework) or macro markers (e.g., expansion vs. recession from official sources) to define regimes.

Rule-based labels have the advantage of transparency and economic interpretability. They are often sufficient to answer first-order questions such as:

> Does this signal survive in both low-vol and high-vol environments, or is it effectively a low-vol carry trade?

Clustering-Based Regimes

When you do not have clear a priori rules, you can let the data suggest regimes through clustering. A common workflow is:

- Choose a set of features describing the environment at each time step: realized volatility, credit spreads, cross-sectional dispersion of returns, liquidity measures (spreads, turnover), correlation levels, and so on.
- Standardize these features to have comparable scales.
- Apply a clustering algorithm (such as k-means or Gaussian mixture models) to group time periods into a small number of clusters.
- Inspect the clusters to understand their characteristics: for example, Cluster 1 might correspond to low-vol, tight spreads, low dispersion; Cluster 2 to high-vol, wide spreads, high dispersion.

You then treat each cluster as a regime and compute performance metrics conditional on cluster membership. The key risk in clustering is over-interpreting noise: if you allow too many clusters or too many noisy features, you may create pseudo-regimes that do not generalize.

Hidden Markov Models (HMMs)

Hidden Markov models add a temporal structure to the clustering idea. They assume that:

- There is an unobserved state (the regime) that evolves over time according to a Markov chain: the next state depends on the current state, not on the full past.

- Observed data (e.g., returns or volatility) are generated from a distribution that depends on the current hidden state.

By fitting an HMM, you learn:

- The typical behaviour of returns in each state (mean, volatility).
- The transition probabilities between states (e.g., how likely a crisis regime is to persist or revert).
- The inferred sequence of regimes over time (or probabilities of being in each regime at each date).

HMMs can be powerful for regime identification and forecasting, but they come with modelling choices and estimation risk. For our purposes, you can treat them as a more formal way of labelling periods into a few states like "normal" and "stressed," then proceed to regime-conditional backtesting.

Regime-Conditional Validation

Once you have regime labels—from rules, clustering, or HMMs—you can transform your validation into a regime-aware exercise:

Compute regime-conditional metrics.

For each regime:

- Compute the signal's IC distribution and average IC.
- Compute the strategy's mean return, volatility, Sharpe ratio, drawdowns, and hit rates.
- Examine turnover, transaction costs, and capacity to see if implementation differs across regimes.

Summarize these in a simple narrative. For instance:

> The signal earns a Sharpe of 1.0 in low-vol regimes, 0.5 in medium-vol regimes, and -0.3 in high-vol regimes. It suffers its worst drawdowns when volatility spikes abruptly.

Check for regime concentration of P&L.

Ask how much of total P&L comes from each regime. A strategy that earns almost all of its profits in one regime but experiences most of its drawdowns in another is structurally fragile, even if its full-sample Sharpe looks decent.

Assess robustness across regimes.

A more robust signal shows:

- Positive or at least non-catastrophic performance across a broad range of regimes.
- Reasonable behaviour when regimes change, without extreme whipsawing or blow-ups.

A fragile signal shows:

- Strong performance in one regime and persistent underperformance or losses in others.
- Sharply deteriorating performance in regimes that are likely to reoccur or lengthen (for example, higher-rate, higher-volatility environments).

This regime-conditional perspective often changes your view of a strategy more than any subtle statistical tweak.

Guardrails and Practical Guidelines

The ultimate goal of regime detection and change-point methods is not to mesmerize with math, but to create *guardrails*: simple rules and checks that prevent you from over-trusting a backtest that is regime-dependent or already obsolete.

Here are practical guidelines:

- **Never trust a single full-sample Sharpe.** Always accompany it with regime-conditional metrics and a narrative of when the strategy earns its keep.

- **Overlay key economic/market events on your diagnostics.** Visual alignment between structural events and breaks in performance is extremely informative.

- **Demand that signals either work across regimes or are explicitly designed to be regime-specific.** If a signal only works in one regime, you must have a view on how often and how long that regime will occur, and what you will do outside it.

- **In live trading, maintain simple regime indicators.** Even if you do not run a full HMM, tracking a few key regime proxies (volatility, spreads, dispersion, credit spreads) can help you judge whether you are in or near the kind of environment the backtest relied on.

- **Use change-point alarms as prompts for review, not automatic switches.** A flagged change-point should trigger a structured review: re-examine signal diagnostics, exposures, and macro context before making portfolio changes.

Regime detection and change-point methods thus extend the idea of alpha half-life from the previous section. Instead of asking only *how fast* a signal decays, you now also ask *under what conditions* it decays or flourishes. In the next section, we will carry this state-aware perspective into the realm of portfolio construction, where risk models, constraints, and scaling choices can interact with regimes in complex ways to reshape the realized alpha of your signals.

5.3 Portfolio Construction Effects on Realized Alpha

In the previous sections we treated signals largely in isolation. We asked whether they decayed over time, and how their performance changed across regimes. In practice, however, no investor trades a bare signal. Every real strategy passes through a portfolio construction pipeline: risk models, hedging rules, scaling schemes, and constraints that turn raw scores into actual positions.

That pipeline is not a neutral conduit. It reshapes, dilutes, and sometimes even reverses your signal's contribution to performance. A strategy can have a clean, intuitive edge at the signal level and still fail in production because the way it is combined with other signals, neutralized, and constrained destroys most of its alpha or explodes its turnover.

This section follows the journey from raw scores to final weights. We will:

- Map the main stages of a typical portfolio construction process.
- Explain how each stage modifies exposures and alters realized alpha.
- Show how diversification, neutralization, and constraints can unintentionally dilute edge and raise trading costs.
- Outline practical habits for diagnosing where in the pipeline a seemingly good signal is being lost.

From Scores to Weights: The Alpha Pipeline

It is useful to fix a mental picture of what happens between a predictive model and the trades that hit the market. Figure sketches a generic pipeline.

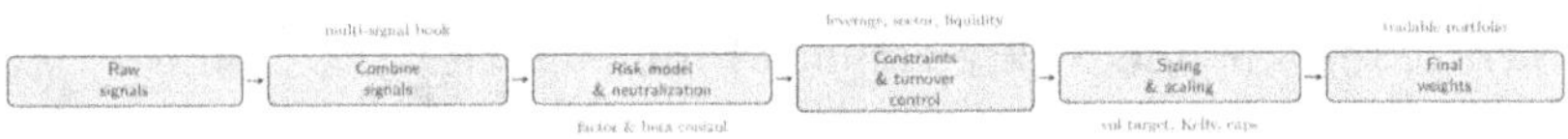

Figure 5.1: **From raw signals to tradable portfolio.** Each stage—signal combination, risk neutralization, constraints, and sizing—modifies exposures and can dilute or reshape realized alpha.

At each stage, we make design choices that trade off risk, turnover, and expected return. The central message of this section is:

> Alpha is not an intrinsic property of a signal alone; it is an emergent property of the entire pipeline that maps that signal into positions under realistic constraints.

To see why, we will now walk through the stages of this pipeline in more detail.

Combining Signals: Diversification vs. Dilution

Most institutional portfolios are driven by multiple signals or factors: value, momentum, quality, carry, sentiment, and so on. Suppose you have a new signal that shows promising information coefficient (IC) and a decent standalone Sharpe when traded as a simple long-short portfolio. The first interaction it faces is with all your existing signals.

Linear combination as a starting point

A basic combination scheme assigns weights to each signal and forms a composite score for each asset. For example:

- Value might get weight 0.5,
- Momentum 0.3,
- Your new signal 0.2.

Assets are then ranked or optimized based on this composite. In a purely linear, unconstrained world with independent signals, adding an uncorrelated positive-alpha signal almost always improves the portfolio's risk-adjusted return.

But we rarely live in that world.

When diversification becomes dilution

Several realistic complications can turn diversification into dilution:

- **Highly correlated signals.** If your new signal is actually a noisy version of an existing one (for example, a slight variation of a momentum definition), the combination may overweight that theme without adding much independent information. The result can be higher risk and turnover for only marginal alpha gain.

- **Opposing signals.** A new signal may systematically disagree with existing ones on certain names. In those cases, signals can cancel each other, shrinking position sizes. If your new signal has weaker standalone edge than the existing ones, it may mostly serve to *dilute* their positions without generating enough incremental alpha to compensate.
- **Capacity and crowding.** Even if a new signal is uncorrelated, it may concentrate on the same capacity-limited names (for example, small illiquid stocks) as other signals. In a constrained portfolio, adding yet another reason to own the same crowded names may not increase net exposures much; instead, it increases sensitivity to trading costs and market impact.

The key lesson is that you should always analyze your signal *in portfolio context*, not just stand-alone. Ask: when combined with everything else, does it still contribute incremental alpha, or does it mostly rearrange or shrink positions?

Risk Models and Neutralization: Necessary Surgery, Real Scars

Risk models enter the pipeline to control exposures to systematic factors (such as the market, sectors, styles, or macro variables) and to forecast covariance matrices for optimization. They also act as filters: when you "neutralize" a signal against risk factors, you remove some of its variation.

Factor-neutrality and signal content

Suppose your signal is positively related to size (it likes small caps) and negatively related to value (it dislikes cheap stocks). If you insist on a portfolio that is neutral to size and value factors, the optimizer will try to offset those exposures.

There are two possible outcomes:

- **Benign neutralization:** The predictive content of your signal is genuinely orthogonal to the factors. Neutralization removes only unintended risk tilts, leaving most of the alpha intact while lowering risk.

- **Destructive neutralization:** The predictive content *is* largely due to a rewarded factor exposure (for example, part of the long-run value premium). Enforcing neutrality then removes much of the alpha itself, leaving behind a weak residual signal and extra turnover from the hedging trades.

This is not a theoretical curiosity. Many "innovative" signals in practice mostly repackage existing style premia. A risk model can expose that by showing strong loadings on standard factors. The difficult decision is whether you want to explicitly own those factor risks or force them out and accept that your signal's net contribution is much smaller than it looked in stand-alone tests.

Risk-only optimizers and unintended outcomes

A typical construction step is "maximize expected return subject to a risk model and constraints." Yet in many shops, the expected returns (alpha forecasts) are small and noisy relative to estimated risk. In that situation, the optimizer tends to behave like a *risk-minimizer with a slight alpha tilt*. Consequences include:

- Portfolios that hug low-risk names even when alpha forecasts point elsewhere.
- Effective dampening of signal strength: differences in expected return across names are heavily shrunk by the desire to keep exposures compact.
- Sensitivity to small changes in inputs: if two names have similar forecasts and risk, minor estimation noise can flip which one the optimizer prefers, generating churn.

If your risk model is overemphasized relative to your alpha, you may end up with a portfolio that is "risk-perfect, alpha-anemic." The raw edge of your signals becomes almost invisible in realized returns.

Constraints: Nonlinear Filters on Alpha

Real portfolios operate under a host of constraints: leverage caps, gross and net exposure limits, position bounds, sector and country limits, style exposure caps, liquidity rules, and turnover budgets. Each constraint is a nonlinear filter that distorts the mapping from signals to weights.

Leverage and exposure limits

Leverage limits cap your ability to scale a signal. If your optimizer wants to take large offsetting long and short positions to exploit small cross-sectional differences in alpha (a common pattern in equity long/short), but you impose a low leverage cap, the optimizer must shrink positions. The result is:

- Lower gross exposure for the same net alpha forecasts.
- A flatter distribution of weights: fewer strong tilts, more mild ones.
- Lower realized Sharpe, even if the signal forecasts were accurate.

Similarly, strict net exposure limits (for example, market-neutrality with tight bands) can force the optimizer to add offsetting positions that are driven by risk control rather than by signals, further diluting alpha.

Position, sector, and country bounds

Position-level and group-level bounds are essential for risk control, but they can strongly interact with signals:

- **Cap on single-name weight.** A strong positive signal on a few names may be capped, forcing capital to spill into second- and third-best ideas. This improves diversification but reduces the contribution of the very best signals.

- **Sector/country limits.** If a signal systematically prefers certain sectors or regions (for good economic reasons), tight caps on those exposures may clip its wings. The optimizer may be forced to find within-sector bets that respect the cap, which may be weaker than cross-sector opportunities the signal originally suggested.

These constraints are particularly binding when a signal is structurally tilted towards certain segments of the universe (for example, small caps, growth stocks, or high-yield bonds). If you choose to own such a signal, you must either relax the relevant constraints or accept that much of its edge will be left on the cutting-room floor.

Turnover controls: trading less, but also earning less

Turnover constraints or penalties aim to reduce trading costs and operational complexity. Common tools include:

- Explicit maximum turnover per period.
- Transaction cost terms in the optimizer's objective function.
- "Holding buffers" that require a minimum signal change before a position is adjusted.

All of these mechanisms effectively *low-pass filter* your signals: they allow only slower, more persistent changes in forecasted alpha to pass through to weights. This is exactly what you want if you are trying to mitigate noise and cost. But if your signal is genuinely short-horizon (with a short alpha half-life), aggressive turnover controls can be fatal: by the time the portfolio reacts, most of the signal has decayed.

Here, the concepts from earlier sections interact tightly: a short half-life signal combined with strict turnover constraints is almost guaranteed to see its realized alpha crushed, even if the raw signal has impressive backtest statistics under frictionless assumptions.

Sizing and Scaling: Volatility Targets and Kelly Temptations

Even after risk control and constraints, you still must decide how large the overall strategy should be and how to allocate risk across signals and time. Sizing and scaling rules further modify realized alpha and risk.

Volatility targeting

A widely used practice is to scale the portfolio such that its forecasted volatility matches a target level (say, 10% annualized). If realized volatility falls, leverage is increased; if volatility rises, leverage is cut.

This has two important effects:

- **Stabilizing risk.** Investors experience a more consistent risk profile over time, which is often a requirement.
- **State-dependent alpha.** If volatility tends to spike in bad regimes for your signal, volatility targeting will automatically scale you down when expected alpha is low, which can be beneficial. However, if your signal actually does well in high-vol regimes, volatility targeting can force you to reduce risk precisely when opportunity is greatest.

As with other design choices, the interaction with regimes is key: the same scaling rule can help or hurt depending on when the signal earns its returns.

Kelly-style and utility-based sizing

In theory, if you know the true distribution of returns, you can compute an "optimal" fraction of capital to allocate to a strategy (for example, via the Kelly criterion or mean-variance utility maximization). In practice, your estimates of alpha and risk are noisy, and these formulas tend to be very aggressive.

Over-aggressive sizing amplifies all of the pipeline's distortions:

- Any mis-estimation of alpha or risk leads to outsized drawdowns.
- Implementation frictions (costs, impact) eat a larger share of returns when you try to push capacity limits.
- Regime shifts or concept drift that reduce alpha temporarily can have permanent capital impacts if you are sized as though the old regime will persist forever.

A conservative approach is to treat theoretical optimal sizing as an upper bound and apply a substantial haircut. In other words, you recognize that the realized alpha of your constructed portfolio will always be worse than the frictionless, noise-free alpha of your backtest.

Why the Same Signal Looks Different in Different Books

At this point, it should be clearer why the same raw signal can have very different realized performance across institutions, or even across strategies within the same firm. Differences in:

- Which other signals it is combined with,
- How risk models neutralize factor exposures,
- How tight constraints are on leverage, sectors, and liquidity,
- How much turnover is allowed,
- And how aggressively risk is scaled over time,

can easily turn a Sharpe 1.0 stand-alone backtest into a Sharpe 0.3 live strategy—or even flip a positive alpha idea into a negative P&L contributor.

This is not just bad luck or exogenous decay. Often, the portfolio construction pipeline itself is the main driver of the gap between model and reality.

Diagnosing Where Alpha Is Lost

To manage these effects, you need diagnostics that trace where in the pipeline your signal's contribution changes. A practical workflow looks like this:

1. **Start with the raw signal.** Measure its IC, standalone long-short portfolio Sharpe, turnover, and capacity under simple rules (e.g., decile portfolios) with basic costs.
2. **Add combination with existing signals.** Recompute metrics for a hypothetical portfolio that uses your true combination scheme but no risk model or constraints. Attribute P&L across signals to see whether your new signal adds incremental alpha or mostly cancels others.
3. **Layer on the risk model and neutralization.** Examine how factor exposures and P&L attribution change. Look for cases where factor-neutralization removes most of the signal's explanatory power.
4. **Introduce constraints and turnover controls.** Simulate or backtest the full set of constraints. Track how often constraints bind for positions driven by your signal, and how much turnover is suppressed.
5. **Apply final sizing and scaling rules.** Assess how state-dependent scaling interacts with the environments in which your signal works or fails.

At each step, compare:

- The marginal contribution of your signal to expected return and realized P&L.
- Its contribution to risk and drawdowns.
- Its induced turnover and transaction costs.

When you see a large drop in contribution from one step to the next, you have found a key point where portfolio construction is reshaping your alpha—often in ways you did not originally intend.

Practical Design Principles

To close, here are some practical principles to keep in mind when designing and evaluating portfolio construction:

- **Align constraints with the signal's nature.** If a signal structurally prefers certain sectors or capitalization buckets, either accept that tilt explicitly or reconsider whether the signal is appropriate for your mandate. Do not blindly neutralize away its core economic content.
- **Match turnover controls to signal horizon.** Short-half-life signals require looser turnover controls and more sophisticated execution; long-horizon signals can support heavier smoothing without excessive alpha loss.
- **Keep risk models honest.** Regularly check whether your risk model is over-dominating the optimizer and turning your alpha portfolio into a risk-minimizer. Consider using shrinkage or simpler models if the alpha is small relative to estimated risk.
- **Benchmark against simple implementations.** Periodically compare your complex optimized portfolio to a simpler construction (e.g., equal-weighted top-minus-bottom deciles). If the complex pipeline delivers only marginally better performance with much higher turnover and complexity, you may be over-engineering.
- **Attribute P&L by stage.** Where possible, maintain P&L attribution not just by signal, but also by construction stage: how much value is added (or lost) by risk hedging, constraints, and scaling decisions.

Viewed through this lens, portfolio construction is not a back-office necessity but a central actor in the drama of model failure. A signal's edge can be eroded by markets learning and regimes shifting, as discussed earlier in the chapter; but it can also be eroded internally, by the very tools we use to make that signal tradable. Understanding and managing this internal decay is just as important as guarding against external decay in the market itself.

5.4 Capacity, Transaction Costs, and Market Impact

The previous section showed that even before you send a single order to the market, portfolio construction can heavily reshape your alpha. In this section we step outside the model and into the market itself. Here, the question is not "Does my signal predict returns in a frictionless backtest?" but rather:

> How much money can I realistically run in this strategy before transaction costs and market impact digest all of its edge?

This question is about *capacity*. Many models fail not because their signals are entirely wrong, but because they are scaled far beyond what the underlying liquidity and market structure can support. Impressive backtests built on small notional sizes or on mid-quote fills turn into fragile, scale-limited trades in production.

Our goals in this section are to:

- Define strategy capacity in intuitive, operational terms.
- Break down the main components of transaction costs and market impact.
- Explain how liquidity, crowding, and self-impact compress alpha as assets under management (AUM) grow.
- Show how to visualize impact-adjusted performance as a function of capital, and how to infer a practical capacity point.

What Do We Mean by Capacity?

At a high level, *capacity* is the amount of capital you can allocate to a strategy such that the expected returns, after all costs, remain attractive relative to risk.

A more precise working definition is:

> Capacity is the level of capital at which the marginal expected net return (after transaction costs and market impact) of deploying an additional dollar into the strategy is zero.

Below capacity, putting in more money still increases expected performance in dollar terms, although often at a diminishing rate. Beyond capacity, each extra unit of capital contributes little or nothing to expected returns, but still adds risk and cost.

Two key features are worth emphasizing:

- Capacity is *strategy-specific*. A slow-moving, diversified, large-cap factor strategy might have billions of dollars of capacity, while a short-horizon, small-cap mean-reversion strategy might saturate at a few million dollars.
- Capacity is *time-varying*. It depends on market liquidity, volatility, crowding by other players, and your own execution quality. A strategy that can trade comfortably in normal times may become capacity-constrained in a crisis when liquidity dries up.

To understand and estimate capacity, we first need to unpack what we mean by costs.

Transaction Costs: Explicit and Implicit

Transaction costs are the friction between your model's theoretical trades and the actual trades executed in the market. They can be grouped into explicit and implicit components.

Explicit costs

These are directly observable charges:

- **Commissions and fees:** Brokerage commissions, exchange fees, clearing and settlement fees, market data, and so on.

- **Taxes and levies:** Stamp duties, transaction taxes, or other jurisdiction-specific charges.

Explicit costs are typically linear in traded volume: if you double the notional traded, you roughly double these costs.

Implicit costs

Implicit costs are more subtle and often more important:

- **Bid-ask spread:** If you aggressively cross the spread (e.g., using market orders), you pay roughly half the spread on each side of the trade, on average.
- **Slippage:** The difference between the price at which you decide to trade (for example, the mid-quote when your signal fired) and the volume-weighted average price at which your order actually fills. It reflects both spread and short-term price movement.
- **Market impact:** The price movement caused by your own trading. Large or urgent orders push prices against you: buy orders tend to lift the price, sell orders to depress it.

While spreads and basic slippage may remain roughly linear with small order sizes, market impact is typically *nonlinear*: as participation increases, each additional unit of volume moves the price more, and the marginal cost per traded dollar rises.

Liquidity and Participation: Why Size Matters

Liquidity is the market's ability to absorb trades without large price moves. For capacity, three quantities are particularly important:

- **Average traded volume:** How many shares or contracts change hands per day in your instruments?
- **Order book depth:** How much size is available near the current price before the order book thins out?

- **Your participation rate:** What fraction of typical daily volume are you trying to trade?

A rule of thumb in many markets is that if you keep your participation rate low (for example, under a few percent of average daily volume per name), you live in a relatively benign impact regime. As you approach or exceed double-digit percentages, impact costs rise sharply. For high-frequency strategies that trade many times a day, effective participation can be even larger on shorter time scales.

Capacity is thus intimately tied to scale:

- For a fixed turnover rate (fraction of the portfolio traded per period), doubling AUM roughly doubles traded volume.
- For fixed universe liquidity, doubling traded volume raises participation rates and, with them, impact costs.

At small sizes, you are a price-taker; at larger sizes, you become a price-maker, moving the market in ways that erode your edges.

Crowding and Self-Impact

Market impact does not come only from your own orders. If many players are running similar strategies, their trades overlap with yours; the market then feels the combined pressure.

External crowding

External crowding occurs when many firms base their trading on similar signals: momentum, carry, volatility selling, or even specific alternative data sets. Consequences include:

- **Compressed spreads and premia:** As more capital chases the same inefficiencies, the ex-ante return premium shrinks. This is another form of signal decay, driven by competition.
- **Elevated impact and unwind risk:** When the trade goes against the crowd (for example, a momentum crash), forced

deleveraging or risk reduction leads to many participants trying to exit positions at the same time, causing large price moves and poor fills.

From a capacity perspective, external crowding reduces the *effective* capacity of a trade. Even if market volume appears large, the fraction safely available to you shrinks when much of it is already implicitly spoken for by others.

Self-impact and feedback loops

Even if you are the only trader using a particular niche signal, your own trading can gradually eat away at the opportunity:

- By repeatedly trading on the same anomaly, you help compress it. For example, systematic buying of undervalued small-cap stocks can bid up their prices, making them less undervalued over time.
- Your order flow may become predictable to sophisticated market makers, who adjust quotes in anticipation, increasing your costs.

This self-impact shortens the effective alpha half-life of your signals: they decay faster *because* you exploit them at scale.

Embedding Costs and Impact into Backtests

Backtests that assume frictionless trading (fills at the mid-price, no impact, no slippage) dramatically overstate performance for any strategy with non-trivial turnover. To get realistic capacity estimates, you must embed cost and impact models directly into the simulation.

Cost models in practice

Common steps include:

- **Estimate spread and fee components:** Use historical quotes and fee schedules to estimate expected costs per share or per notional traded, by asset and over time.

- **Model impact as a function of order size and liquidity:** For example, specify impact in basis points as increasing with the square root (or another concave function) of the participation rate. The exact form can be calibrated from your own execution data.
- **Apply costs to simulated trades:** For each trade in the backtest, subtract the estimated cost from P&L. This produces cost-adjusted performance metrics.

Once costs are embedded, you can run backtests at different capital levels by scaling position sizes and thus traded volume. As AUM increases, so do participation and impact costs.

Impact-adjusted capacity curves

For each hypothetical capital level, you can compute:

- **Net P&L:** The expected or realized profit after all embedded costs.
- **Marginal Sharpe or marginal return:** The incremental risk-adjusted performance associated with a small increase in capital around that level.

Plotting these quantities against capital creates an *impact-adjusted capacity curve* that summarizes how scaling affects performance.

Right after we define these ideas, it is helpful to see an illustrative picture.

In this stylized chart, net P&L initially rises with capital, then flattens, and eventually declines as impact and costs dominate. The marginal Sharpe (or marginal return) declines steadily and crosses zero at the *capacity point*: beyond this, additional capital does not increase net performance.

Interpreting the Capacity Curve

Capacity curves convey several useful insights:

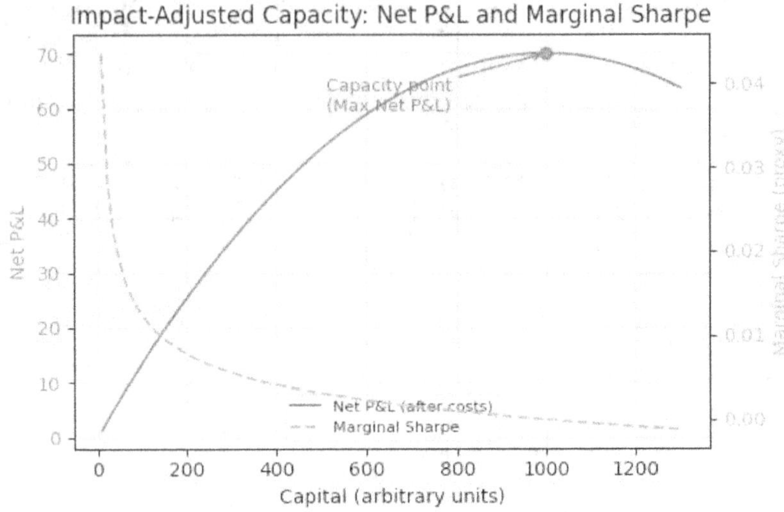

- **Diminishing returns zone:** Even before you hit capacity, you may enter a region where net P&L still rises with capital but at a sharply declining rate. If you are paid on Sharpe or information ratio, this zone may already be unattractive.

- **Capacity point:** Where marginal Sharpe is near zero, or where net P&L flattens. This is a natural upper bound on economically sensible scale.

- **Overloaded regime:** If you push capital far beyond capacity, total net P&L can actually *decline*, and your realized Sharpe falls substantially. In this region, you are mostly enriching your broker and liquidity providers.

In real life, the curve is estimated with error, and capacity is not a single precise number but a range. It is prudent to operate comfortably *below* the best estimate of capacity, both to allow for uncertainty and to reduce sensitivity to liquidity shocks or regime changes.

Why High-Turnover and Small-Cap Strategies Are Fragile

Some strategies are far more sensitive to costs and impact than others.

High-turnover strategies

For high-frequency or short-horizon strategies, turnover can reach hundreds or even thousands of percent per year. Each basis point of cost directly eats away at expected return. A strategy with a theoretical gross Sharpe of 3 before costs might end up with a net Sharpe below 1 after realistic slippage and impact.

Three compounding effects hurt such strategies:

- **Decay and delay:** Signals with very short half-lives lose much of their value if execution is slightly delayed or if queue priority is lost.
- **Cost scaling:** Because of high turnover, even small per-trade costs accumulate quickly over the year.
- **Capacity compression:** The more often you trade, the more frequently you interact with the order book, increasing the effective participation rate on short time scales.

As a result, high-frequency edges can be both extremely profitable at very small scale *and* extremely capacity-limited. Scaling them is like trying to pour the ocean into a bottle: the bottleneck is not the backtest, but the market's ability to absorb your orders.

Small-cap and illiquid strategies

Strategies focused on small-cap or otherwise illiquid securities face a different, but related, set of constraints:

- Average daily volume in these names is often low, and quoted depth thin. Even modest absolute trade sizes can represent large fractions of daily volume.

- Spreads are wider, and volatility is higher, making each basis point of alpha harder to capture net of costs.
- External crowding can arrive quickly: if several funds discover similar anomalies in the same small universe, they rapidly exhaust the available liquidity.

These characteristics compress capacity. A signal that looks incredibly attractive on paper—because price moves are large relative to noise—may only support a few million dollars of capital before costs overwhelm returns.

Scaling Paths and Scenario Analysis

Capacity is not only about the final scale; it is also about *how* you get there. A prudent scaling path involves:

- **Gradual increases in capital:** Incrementally raise AUM, monitor net performance and execution quality, and stop or reverse if marginal returns deteriorate faster than expected.
- **Scenario analysis:** Before scaling, simulate how the strategy would behave under stressed liquidity conditions (for example, spreads doubling, volumes halving). This gives you a sense of how much capital would still be manageable in bad times.
- **Dynamic size adjustments:** Consider adjusting capital allocated to capacity-sensitive strategies based on current liquidity metrics and realized costs, rather than keeping size fixed.

Scenario analysis can be performed in backtests by artificially changing cost parameters or limiting traded volume to mimic adverse conditions. If a strategy's economics fall apart under mild stress, it is a warning sign that true capacity is low.

Practical Heuristics and Guardrails

Estimating capacity with high precision requires detailed execution data and careful modelling. However, a few practical heuristics can help keep you out of the most dangerous zones:

- **Participation caps:** Impose hard caps on your participation in daily volume per name (for example, 5% in normal markets, lower in stressed conditions).
- **Turnover-aware sizing:** Reduce allocated capital as turnover rises; for example, a high-turnover variant of a strategy runs at smaller notional than a low-turnover variant with similar pre-cost Sharpe.
- **Cost-to-alpha ratio checks:** For each strategy and capital level, compare estimated annualized costs to expected gross alpha. If costs exceed a comfortable fraction (say, 30–50%) of gross alpha, you are near or beyond sensible capacity.
- **Execution quality monitoring:** Track realized slippage and impact over time. Sudden degradations, especially when not explained by volatility or regime shifts, may indicate that you or others are pushing capacity limits.
- **Diversification of liquidity sources:** Spread trades across venues, time, and instruments when possible, to reduce concentrated impact in any single order book or time slice.

These guardrails will not give a single magic number for capacity, but they significantly reduce the risk of scaling a strategy to the point where it quietly turns from a portfolio alpha source into a transaction-cost engine.

From Backtest Edge to Real-World Scale

Capacity, transaction costs, and market impact form the bridge between model performance and real-world profitability. A common pattern in failed strategies is:

- A strong signal is discovered and validated in small-scale, frictionless backtests.
- Portfolio construction and risk controls attenuate the edge, but performance still looks acceptable.

- The strategy is scaled aggressively, often to satisfy AUM growth targets.
- Liquidity limits, crowding, and self-impact drag realized returns down until the net strategy becomes mediocre or unprofitable.

By explicitly quantifying costs and impact, embedding them into backtests, and visualizing impact-adjusted capacity curves, you can interrupt this pattern. Instead of asking "How high is the Sharpe?" you ask:

> At what scale, in which markets, and under which liquidity conditions does this model actually deliver that Sharpe?

In the final section of the chapter we turn to the last piece of the puzzle: execution. There we will see how microstructure details, order choice, and latency affect implementation shortfall, and why strategies with short alpha half-lives are especially vulnerable to any inefficiency in the way you get from desired weights to actual trades.

5.5 Execution Quality, Slippage, and Latency

The previous sections focused on how signals decay, how regimes change, and how portfolio construction and capacity reshape theoretical alpha. In all of that analysis, we quietly assumed that when the model decides to buy or sell, the trade occurs at roughly the price used in the backtest.

In live markets this assumption is almost never true. Between the moment your model computes desired weights and the moment your orders complete, you pass through the microstructure layer: order books, queues, spreads, and other traders. The losses that occur along this "last mile" are grouped under *execution costs*, and the gap between the model's notional P&L and realized P&L is called *implementation shortfall.*

For slow-moving, high-capacity strategies, moderate execution inefficiency may merely trim the edges of performance. For fast-decaying, short-horizon signals, it is often fatal: a few basis points of extra slippage, or a few hundred milliseconds of extra latency, can destroy most of the expected alpha before the trade completes.

In this section we:

- Define implementation shortfall and its main components.
- Explain how order choice (market vs. limit, passive vs. aggressive) interacts with microstructure to create or mitigate slippage.
- Highlight why latency and queue position matter particularly for fast-decaying signals.
- Offer practical guidelines for aligning execution design with signal half-life, volatility, and capacity.

From Theoretical P&L to Implementation Shortfall

When you run a backtest, you implicitly choose a *benchmark price* at which you assume trades occur: most often the close, open, or bar mid-price. Implementation shortfall measures how much performance you lose relative to this idealized benchmark when you trade in the real market.

A simple verbal definition is:

> Implementation shortfall is the difference between the P&L you would have earned if all trades happened at the model's benchmark prices and the P&L you actually earn at your realized execution prices.

This gap can be decomposed into several components:

- **Spread cost:** Paying the bid-ask spread when you cross the market.
- **Delay cost:** Adverse price moves between signal time and execution time, even if you eventually trade at the then-current mid.

- **Impact cost:** Price moves caused by your own order, especially if it is large or aggressive.
- **Missed trades and partial fills:** Situations where you do not get the desired size, or get it too late, and therefore miss part of the modeled opportunity.

Even if you think of yourself as a "long-term investor," ignoring these components can bias your assessment of alpha, especially when signals are more short-term than you realize, or when you operate near capacity limits.

A Quick Tour of Market Microstructure

To understand execution quality, we need a basic picture of how modern electronic markets work. At a high level:

- Traders submit *limit orders* specifying a price and size, or *market orders* that ask to trade immediately at the best available prices.
- The limit order book collects and sorts outstanding limit orders by price and time. At the top on each side are the best bid (highest buy price) and best ask (lowest sell price).
- The *spread* is the difference between best ask and best bid. The *mid-price* is their average.
- When a market order arrives, it "walks the book," consuming resting liquidity starting at the best prices and moving outward if the order is large.

Three microstructure concepts are especially relevant for execution:

- **Depth:** The amount of liquidity (shares, contracts) available at or near the current price. Thin depth means that even a moderate order moves the price.
- **Queue position:** For a given price level, limit orders are filled in time order. Being early in the queue increases your chance of getting filled without having to cross the spread.

- **Hidden and dark liquidity:** Some orders are not visible in the top-of-book quotes (for example, iceberg or dark-pool orders) but can still provide fills.

Your execution decisions determine how you interact with this structure: whether you mostly take liquidity (market orders, aggressive limits) or provide it (passive limits), how long you are willing to wait, and how exposed you are to adverse moves while waiting.

Order Choice: Immediacy vs. Price

The simplest execution decision is choosing between market and limit orders.

Market orders: Certainty of execution, uncertain price

A market order is an instruction to trade immediately at the best available prices. Its characteristics are:

- **Pros:** High certainty of execution and speed. You quickly realize your desired position, which is particularly valuable when alpha decays rapidly or when you must rebalance to meet risk constraints.
- **Cons:** You almost always pay the full spread, and for larger orders, you may also pay significant impact as the order walks through the book. Your realized price can be notably worse than the mid-quote at the time you sent the order.

Backtests that assume execution at the mid underestimate costs of market orders by roughly half the spread per side, which is material for high-turnover strategies or in assets with wide spreads.

Limit orders: Price control, uncertain execution

A limit order specifies a maximum (for buys) or minimum (for sells) price at which you are willing to trade. Key characteristics:

- **Pros:** You can avoid crossing the spread by posting at or inside the current best quotes. If your order gets filled passively, you save spread costs and may even earn the spread.

- **Cons:** Execution is uncertain and may be delayed. If the market moves away from your limit, you might not trade at all, or you may need to "chase" the price with new orders, losing both time and price.

For slow-decaying signals, missing or delaying some trades might be acceptable if it meaningfully reduces average costs. For fast-decaying signals, waiting too long can be worse than paying the spread: the price may move against you simply because the alpha is being realized while you sit in the queue.

Execution algorithms: Blends of market and limit logic

In practice, most institutional trading uses execution algorithms that mix market and limit behaviour:

- **VWAP (Volume-Weighted Average Price):** Schedules trades over time in proportion to historical or predicted volume patterns, often using limit orders and mild aggression. It aims to match or beat the day's volume-weighted price.

- **TWAP (Time-Weighted Average Price):** Trades at a steady pace over a chosen interval, regardless of volume. Used when the main objective is to avoid information leakage or timing risk relative to a specific horizon.

- **Participation algorithms (POV):** Target a fixed participation rate (e.g., 10% of market volume) and adjust order submission dynamically as volume evolves. Helpful for large orders where impact must be controlled.

- **Opportunistic and smart routers:** Use short-term signals about order book state and venue conditions to decide where and how to post or take liquidity.

All of these strategies trade off immediacy, price risk, and information leakage. The right choice depends heavily on your signal's half-life and the strength of your alpha forecast.

Latency and Fast-Decaying Signals

In earlier sections, we introduced alpha half-life: the time over which the predictive power of a signal decays by half. For many short-horizon strategies, this half-life can be intraday, or even measured in minutes or seconds.

In such settings, *latency*—the elapsed time between signal generation and execution—becomes a primary determinant of whether any alpha is captured.

Latency has multiple components:

- Time to compute the signal or update the model.
- Network and communication delays between your systems and the exchange or broker.
- Time in the broker's or exchange's internal queues.
- Wait time in the order book before a limit order is filled.

Consider a simple illustration:

- A signal has a half-life of 5 minutes.
- Your round-trip latency from signal to trade completion is also about 5 minutes on average.

By the time you complete a typical trade, the expected alpha associated with that signal snapshot has already decayed by about half; in volatile or competitive markets, it may be worse. If implementation shortfall and latency together consume more than the expected alpha, the strategy may still look good in a backtest that assumed instantaneous execution, but it will fail in production.

For high-frequency strategies, technical details that seem mundane in other contexts—co-location, optimized code paths, kernel bypass, order-entry throttles—directly translate into real money. A small latency disadvantage versus competitors who trade on similar signals can mean you are systematically late to the opportunity, trading on stale information and suffering adverse selection.

Adverse Selection and Information Leakage

Adverse selection is the flip side of providing liquidity: when your limit orders are filled, it might be precisely because someone else has better information and is happy to trade against you.

From a model perspective:

- If you post passive limit orders without conditioning on your own signal, you might systematically trade in the wrong direction when your signal indicates that short-term pressure is against you.
- If your signal is widely used (e.g., simple momentum), liquidity providers may adjust spreads or "fade" quotes in anticipation of the typical trading pattern, increasing your costs.

Information leakage exacerbates adverse selection. Large, predictable execution patterns—for example, always trading at the close, or slicing large orders naively over the day—can be detected and front-run by others, who then profit from your impact. Reducing this leakage by randomizing execution, varying tactics, or using less predictable schedules can meaningfully improve realized performance.

Aligning Execution to Signal Horizon

A central design principle is that *execution style must be matched to the signal's effective horizon and strength.* Some guidelines, moving from short- to long-horizon signals, are:

Very short-horizon signals (intra-day, minutes to hours)

- **Priority:** Minimize latency and timing risk, even at the cost of paying spreads and some impact.
- **Order choice:** More aggressive; frequent use of market or near-marketable limit orders. The main risk is not trading in time.
- **Execution window:** Narrow. Many strategies must complete trades within a small fraction of the signal half-life.

- **Monitoring:** Fine-grained analysis of slippage versus short-term price moves; continuous tuning of tactics.

If your backtest assumes that these trades occur at mid-prices but your real execution often lags by even a few seconds or by a few ticks of price movement, the realized alpha can vanish.

Medium-horizon signals (daily to weekly)

- **Priority:** Balance between cost control and timing risk. Some delay is acceptable if it substantially reduces spreads and impact.
- **Order choice:** Mix of passive and aggressive orders; use of VWAP/TWAP or participation algos tuned to typical holding periods.
- **Execution window:** Hours to a trading day. It is often better to spread trades to avoid clustering impact if alpha decays only slowly over this window.
- **Monitoring:** Compare performance of different execution tactics over similar signals and market conditions; adapt based on realized cost profiles.

Here, the backtest should at least incorporate realistic assumptions about which part of the day you trade (e.g., volume-weighted prices) and about typical spreads and slippage.

Long-horizon signals (monthly and beyond)

- **Priority:** Minimize costs and allow flexibility. Implementation shortfall is still important but less sensitive to minute-level timing.
- **Order choice:** Heavier use of passive liquidity, opportunistic execution, and crossing networks; strong emphasis on spread capture and impact avoidance.
- **Execution window:** Multiple days or weeks as needed, provided that allocation and risk limits are respected.

- **Monitoring:** Focus on aggregate cost per turnover cycle; ensure that execution does not introduce unintended timing biases (for example, always trading in low-liquidity windows).

For such strategies, naive execution can still waste a meaningful share of annual alpha, but the constraint is more on cost minimization than on beating ultra-fast competitors.

Measuring Execution Quality

To manage execution, you must measure it. Common post-trade analytics include:

- **Shortfall versus benchmark:** For each order or basket, compare realized average execution price to a benchmark (arrival price, open, close, VWAP). Decompose differences into spread, timing, and impact components where possible.
- **Slippage distributions:** Track the distribution of slippage (in basis points) by asset, order size, time of day, and tactic. Identify patterns where certain combinations systematically perform worse.
- **Fill ratios and missed trades:** Monitor how often and how fully limit orders fill at different limit offsets and queue positions. Chronic non-fills may indicate that your price expectations are unrealistic or that you are being adverse-selected.
- **Cost versus volatility:** Relate realized costs to contemporaneous volatility and volume. Costs that spike disproportionately relative to volatility may highlight capacity issues or poor execution choices.

Crucially, you should feed this information back into your models. If, for instance, you learn that a given asset or time-of-day is consistently expensive to trade, you might:

- Adjust signals or portfolio construction to reduce unnecessary turnover in those contexts.

- Incorporate execution cost forecasts directly into position-sizing decisions.

Execution as Part of the Model, Not an Afterthought

Throughout this chapter we have seen that apparent alpha can be eroded by many forces: concept drift, regime shifts, portfolio construction, capacity limits, and now execution frictions. A common failure mode is to treat execution as something that happens "downstream" from the model, to be handled by a separate team or a generic broker algorithm.

For robust strategies, the integration must be tighter:

- **Model-aware execution:** Execution tactics that adapt to the current strength and horizon of your signal (for example, trading more aggressively on high-conviction, short-lived signals; more patiently on low-turnover, long-lived ones).
- **Execution-aware models:** Signals and portfolio construction processes that are built with realistic assumptions about fill prices, delays, and costs from the outset, not retrofitted later.
- **Closed feedback loops:** Regular comparison of modeled and realized implementation shortfall, with iterative adjustments to both model and execution to reduce systematic gaps.

For fast-decaying signals in particular, execution is effectively part of the alpha engine: the line between "signal generation" and "execution" blurs. The edge is not simply in forecasting where prices will be, but in *being able to trade on that forecast* before it decays, at a price that leaves some of the forecasted return in your pocket.

If the earlier parts of this chapter taught us to be skeptical of backtests that ignore decay, regimes, and capacity, this section adds a final caution: be equally skeptical of backtests that pretend trading occurs at idealized prices. A model that survives concept drift, regime shifts, portfolio constraints, and capacity limits can still fail if its designers neglect the last mile—where the market, not the model, has the final word.

Chapter 6

Governance, Monitoring, and Model Lifecycle

Most quants obsess over Sharpe ratios and signal discovery, but the trades that survive contact with the market are usually the ones protected by process. This chapter argues that model failure is not just a statistical accident-it is an operational risk that can be governed, audited, and monitored like any other. We will design a lightweight but rigorous model lifecycle: clear ownership and challenge, reproducible research, production-grade monitoring, and systematic refresh policies that accept signal decay as inevitable and manage it on your terms rather than the market's.

6.1 Model Risk Governance and Controls

Up to this point we have treated overfitting, leakage, and signal decay mainly as technical problems. In practice, they are just as much *governance* problems. Most catastrophic model failures in trading do not happen because no one on the team understood cross-validation; they happen because no one was clearly accountable, no one had the authority to say "stop," or the organization quietly rewarded corner-cutting.

This section reframes model risk as something that must be managed through clear roles, challenge rights, and hard guardrails. We will answer three concrete questions:

- Who *owns* each model?
- Who is allowed—indeed, encouraged—to *challenge* it?
- Which *controls* prevent research shortcuts from leaking into production?

The goal is not bureaucracy for its own sake. Good governance makes it institutionally difficult to ship fragile, overfit models, and it makes it obvious what to do when live performance diverges from expectations.

What Is Model Risk in a Trading Context?

Before defining roles, it helps to be explicit about what we are trying to control. In a trading environment, *model risk* is the risk of loss or damage arising because a model is wrong, misused, or misunderstood. It shows up in several ways:

- **P&L volatility and losses**: The most visible form. An overfit signal that looked great in backtests suddenly posts a severe drawdown once live.
- **Hidden tail exposures**: A model that was calibrated only on benign regimes may be implicitly short volatility or liquidity. When markets gap, losses are far worse than the backtest suggested.
- **Operational errors**: Bugs, misconfigured parameters, stale data, or dropped corporate actions can quietly distort trades without immediately triggering risk limits.
- **Reputational and regulatory damage**: If a firm cannot explain how its models make decisions, regulators, investors,

and internal stakeholders lose confidence, especially after a loss event.

A common pattern is that these failures are not detected early because no one is explicitly responsible for asking: "Is this model still behaving as expected?" Good governance assigns that responsibility and defines how it can be challenged.

Model Ownership: One Name on the Door

Every production model should have a single clear *owner*. In small teams the owner might be a portfolio manager (PM) who also codes; in larger organizations it is often the lead PM or a designated "strategy owner." The precise title is less important than the clarity: for each live model, you should be able to write on one line:

Model X → Owned by: Alice Smith

The owner is not necessarily the original researcher. People leave, models get inherited, and research is often collaborative. Ownership is about *ongoing accountability*, not intellectual credit.

Responsibilities of the Model Owner

The model owner is accountable for the following:

- **Understanding**: Being able to explain, in plain language, what the model does, where its edge is believed to come from, and under which conditions it is expected to perform or fail.
- **Risk profile**: Knowing the model's risk limits, typical drawdown profile, and key sensitivities (e.g., factor exposures, liquidity assumptions).
- **Deployment decisions**: Deciding when to deploy, scale up, scale down, or decommission the model, subject to approval processes described below.
- **Monitoring response**: Responding to alerts and breaches in post-deployment monitoring, coordinating investigation and remedial actions.

- **Documentation**: Ensuring that the model card, assumptions, and validation evidence are complete and up to date.

The owner *does not* have unilateral power to do whatever they want. Ownership works alongside a separation of duties and an independent challenge function.

A Simple Governance Structure: Roles and Separation of Duties

In most quant trading organizations, four functions repeatedly appear around the model lifecycle:

- **Researcher**: Designs signals, features, and models; runs backtests; proposes changes.
- **Portfolio Manager (PM)**: Owns the P&L, decides capital allocation, and usually serves as model owner.
- **Model Risk / Validation**: An independent function that reviews models, interrogates assumptions, and can block deployment.
- **Operations / Technology**: Implements and runs the model in production, maintains data feeds and infrastructure.

To avoid both confusion and conflicts of interest, you want a clear *RACI-style* assignment of responsibilities across key lifecycle steps:

- **Design**
- **Backtest**
- **Validation**
- **Approval**
- **Deployment**
- **Review**

"RACI" is a simple governance tool that labels each role as:

- *R*esponsible: does the work.
- *A*ccountable: ultimately answerable; there is exactly one "A" per task.
- *C*onsulted: gives input.
- *I*nformed: kept up to date, but not directly involved.

A crisp RACI matrix reduces handoff errors and makes it harder for one enthusiastic team to push through a fragile model without independent scrutiny.

Diagrammatic representation:

Lifecycle Step	Researcher	Portfolio Manager	Model Risk	Operations
Design	R	A/C	C	I
Backtest	R	A/C	C	I
Validation	C	C	R/A	I
Approval	C	A	R/C	I
Deployment	I	C	C	R/A
Review	C	A	R	R

R: Responsible, **A**: Accountable, **C**: Consulted, **I**: Informed. Single 'A' per step; Model Risk remains independent from PM/Researcher.

This sort of matrix is only a starting point; you should adapt it to your specific organization. The key features to preserve are:

- Exactly one **accountable** party per lifecycle step.
- **Independence** of the Model Risk function from the PM and Research teams.
- **Operational separation** between those who design models and those who deploy and run them.

Who May Challenge a Model, and How?

Healthy model governance explicitly defines a *right to challenge*. Without this, cultural pressure tends to suppress dissent: no one wants to be the person who delays a promising strategy.

There are three main challenge channels:

1. Model Risk / Validation as Formal Challenger

The Model Risk or Validation team is tasked with formal, structured challenge. Typical activities include:

- Reproducing key backtests independently using frozen data and code.
- Stress-testing the model under extreme but plausible scenarios.
- Checking for data issues: survivorship bias, look-ahead, snooping, misaligned timestamps.
- Questioning the economic story and robustness of the signal: Why should this edge persist? What could erode it?

They have the authority to issue conditions, such as: "Deployment only with half the proposed leverage," or "Deployment only after this additional stress test is passed."

2. Peer Challenge within Research and Portfolio Teams

Researchers and PMs should be encouraged to critique each other's work through:

- Internal seminars where new models are presented.
- Code and methodology reviews.
- Red-team exercises where a colleague tries to "break" the result by changing assumptions, data samples, or costs.

This informal challenge is powerful precisely because the challenger understands the modeling context deeply.

3. Operational and Data Challenge

Operations and data teams often notice issues first: strange order sizes, mismatched timestamps, sudden spikes in missing data. They must have:

- Clearly documented **escalation paths** to alert PMs and Model Risk.
- The authority to **halt** a model's trading in the face of serious operational anomalies, even if the PM has not yet approved.

Documented Challenge Outcomes

Challenges must leave a paper trail. For every major model, you should be able to show:

- What concerns were raised.
- How they were addressed (or why they were accepted as residual risk).
- Who signed off on proceeding.

This is essential later when performance diverges from expectations: you can distinguish between genuinely unforeseen events and risks that were consciously accepted.

Guardrails Against Research Shortcuts

Even with the best intentions, researchers under performance pressure will be tempted to "massage" results. Effective governance uses *guardrails* so that such shortcuts are either impossible or easily detected. Think of guardrails in three layers: data, testing protocol, and stress/approval requirements.

Data Quality and Access Controls

Many overfitting and leakage issues trace back to informal, poorly controlled data work. Basic data governance includes:

- **Centralized, curated datasets**: Official "golden" datasets for prices, fundamentals, and reference data, with known cleaning rules and versioning. Ad-hoc spreadsheets or local CSVs should not feed production models.

- **Write protection for production data**: Researchers can query and transform views, but not modify canonical production data directly.
- **Provenance tracking**: For each feature used by a model, there should be a clear description of its source, any vendor adjustments, and transformation steps.

These practices make it harder for accidental data snooping or silent data corruption to slip into a model.

Mandatory Out-of-Sample Testing

A core guardrail against overfitting is a *non-negotiable* out-of-sample testing regime, with policies such as:

- **Predefined evaluation windows**: Before seeing results, define which periods will be used for training, validation, and final testing. Changing these later requires justification and sign-off.
- **Hold-out or rolling windows**: Reserve a hold-out period or use walk-forward validation to mimic the live deployment process.
- **No peeking at test results while iterating**: Researchers can iterate freely on training and validation sets, but should not repeatedly inspect test performance to guide tweaks. In practice, this can be enforced by having Model Risk control access to the final test results or by logging all evaluations on the hold-out set.

The objective is not to outlaw exploration but to ensure that performance claims rely on genuinely unseen data, not repeatedly mined test sets.

Prohibited Shortcut Practices

Some practices are so consistently harmful that they should simply be prohibited for production-bound research:

- **Using future information**: Any use of knowledge from $t + 1$ or later in features, labels, or filters at time t (e.g., filtering stocks on full-year earnings known only later).
- **Survivorship-biased universes**: Backtests based only on the set of assets alive today, without delisting or delisted securities.
- **Parameter fishing without penalties**: Trying large grids of parameters and picking the best-performing combination without any complexity penalty, multiple-testing control, or robustness checks.
- **Ad hoc exclusion of "bad" periods**: Dropping inconvenient crash periods or other adverse regimes from the backtest without a compelling, documented economic reason.

A robust governance framework makes such shortcuts visible during validation and blocks models that rely on them.

Required Stress and Scenario Analyses

Before deployment, models should be subjected to standardized stress tests that are part of the approval checklist, not optional extras. Typical requirements include:

- **Historical event replay**: How would the model have behaved around major stress events (e.g., 2008 crisis, sudden liquidity shocks), adjusted as needed to respect realistic data availability at the time?
- **Factor shocks**: What happens if key risk factors move sharply (e.g., value, momentum, volatility, rates)? Are exposures within risk appetite?
- **Liquidity and cost shocks**: How sensitive is the strategy to wider spreads, slippage, or reduced market depth?

The aim is to uncover non-linearities and hidden tail risks that might not be obvious from typical in-sample metrics like Sharpe ratios.

Approval Workflows: From Proposal to Production

Putting all of the above together, a new model or major change should follow a structured approval process. One practical template:

- **Research Proposal**: Researcher and PM document the idea, economic rationale, data, preliminary backtests, and expected role in the portfolio.
- **Preliminary Review**: Model Risk and Operations give early feedback on feasibility, data needs, and operational complexity.
- **Full Validation Package**: The team produces the model card, detailed backtests (with out-of-sample results), stress tests, and implementation specs.
- **Independent Validation**: Model Risk replicates key results, checks for biases and shortcuts, and issues a validation opinion (approve, approve with conditions, or reject).
- **Formal Approval**: A risk or investment committee, including the PM and Model Risk, signs off on deployment scope (capital, leverage, markets) and any conditions.
- **Controlled Deployment**: Operations rolls out the model according to a runbook, often with phased capital and heightened monitoring in an initial period.

Blocking and Conditional Approval

Critically, the governance framework must give Model Risk and certain committees *real veto power*, not just advisory status. Examples:

- Model Risk can block deployment if validation reveals unreconciled inconsistencies, unfixable data issues, or reliance on prohibited shortcuts.
- Approval can be conditional, for example limiting risk exposure until sufficient live data accumulates, or requiring specific additional tests within a set timeframe.

Without such teeth, validation devolves into box-ticking, and overfit models will reach production.

How Governance Reduces Overfitting and Signal Decay Risk

It may be tempting to see all these processes as overhead. In reality, good governance directly addresses the core themes of this book:

- **Overfitting**: Mandatory out-of-sample tests, independent replication, and prohibitions on data shortcuts make it harder to "optimize on noise" without being caught.
- **Signal decay**: Clear ownership and review responsibilities ensure that someone is watching for deterioration relative to expectations, not just reacting after a large drawdown.
- **Learning from failure**: Documentation of assumptions and challenge history turns each failure into a learning opportunity. You can trace back which risks were known, which were missed, and adjust your standards.
- **Institutional memory**: As people move on, the combination of model cards, validation reports, and approval decisions preserves knowledge about what has been tried and why certain approaches were rejected.

Ultimately, governance is about aligning incentives and information. When every model has a clearly named owner, an empowered challenger, and strict controls on how research gets promoted to production, you turn model risk from an amorphous fear into a manageable part of the trading business.

6.2 Documentation, Audit, and Change Control

In the previous section we treated model governance as a question of roles, accountability, and guardrails. We answered: who owns each model, who may challenge it, and which approval steps stand between a backtest and live trading. This section turns to a more mundane but equally decisive question: *what is actually written down* about the model, and how its many moving parts are versioned and audited over time.

Most model disasters share two depressing features:

- No one can reconstruct precisely what model, data, or parameters were live when the losses occurred.
- Even if they could, there is no clear record of the model's original assumptions and limitations, so the post-mortem becomes guesswork.

The result is that the same mistakes are repeated, and it remains impossible to tell whether an apparent failure is due to genuine signal decay, a coding bug, or an undocumented change in data handling.

Disciplined documentation and change control aim to avoid this. They transform models from opaque spreadsheets into *auditable, reproducible systems.* We will proceed in three steps:

- Introduce the idea of a *model card* or specification document.
- Explain practical *versioning and change control* for code, data, and configuration.
- Show how an audit trail allows you to distinguish implementation errors from real economic failure, and to learn from model retirements.

Throughout, the focus remains on accessibility: the goal is not to produce legal-style documents no one reads, but to make the model intelligible to an informed outsider.

From Opaque Tool to Described Object: The Model Card

Think of a typical spreadsheet-based trading strategy you might encounter in a small fund: a workbook with dozens of tabs, some hard-coded constants, data pulled from a vendor feed, and a final column labelled "signal." If the person who built it disappears, it is very hard to answer basic questions such as:

- What is the strategy *trying* to do?
- Which data fields, exactly, does it rely on?
- How was performance tested?
- Under what conditions is it expected to break?

A *model card* is a structured document that answers these questions in a consistent format for every model. It is not a marketing slide deck; it is written for a skeptical but intelligent reader who was not involved in the research. At a minimum, a useful model card contains:

1. Purpose and Economic Rationale

This is the one-paragraph answer to "what is this model for?" and "why should it work?" Examples:

- "This model is a medium-horizon equity value strategy, aiming to capture mean reversion in valuation ratios over 6–18 months."
- "This model is an intraday futures spread strategy, exploiting short-lived mispricings between correlated contracts."

The rationale should connect to an economic story (risk premium, behavioral bias, structural market feature), not just a statistical pattern such as "the regression coefficient is significant."

2. Scope and Role in the Portfolio

Here you specify:

- Asset classes and markets traded.
- Target holding periods and turnover.
- Typical position sizes and gross/net exposures.
- Intended role: alpha source, hedge, diversifier, liquidity provider, and so on.

This information helps later when assessing whether the model is being used as intended.

3. Data Inputs and Provenance

This is one of the most important sections. For each data input or feature family, the card should state:

- Data vendor and product name.
- Field names or definitions (e.g., "split- and dividend-adjusted close price"; "12-month trailing EPS").
- Frequency and history (e.g., daily back to 1995; quarterly back to 1980).
- Any known quirks: lag in reporting, restatements, survivorship issues, missingness patterns.

If internal data is used (such as proprietary execution quality measures, internal risk factors, or order book reconstructions), the card should name the owning team and link to their own specification.

The aim is that an auditor could, in principle, reconstruct the exact dataset the model expects, without reverse-engineering code.

4. Feature Definitions

Features are the derived quantities the model actually uses, such as momentum scores, valuation ratios, volatility estimates, or machine learning embeddings. For each feature, a good model card includes:

- A plain-language description (e.g., "12-month price momentum, skipping the last month").
- A mathematical or algorithmic definition (if simple enough) or a reference to the module that computes it.
- Any data filters or winsorization rules (e.g., "winsorized at 1st and 99th percentile cross-sectionally").
- Update frequency and lookback window.

You do not need to reproduce pages of code, but you should give enough detail that a competent quant could recreate the feature from the described inputs.

5. Training, Validation, and Backtest Regime

This section summarizes how the model was developed and tested:

- Sample periods for training, validation, and testing.
- Cross-validation or walk-forward procedures, if used.
- Performance metrics tracked (e.g., Sharpe ratio, hit rate, drawdown statistics).
- Any hyperparameter tuning process and how overfitting was controlled.

The emphasis is on the *process*, not the prettiest Sharpe you obtained.

6. Assumptions and Limitations

Here you list what the model *expects* about the world:

- Typical levels of transaction costs and market impact.
- Assumptions about liquidity and trade sizes.
- Stability of certain correlations or factor structures.
- Operational assumptions (e.g., "all orders must be executed by close"; "no trading on days with exchange holidays in region X").

You also state known weaknesses:

- Sensitivity to sudden volatility spikes.
- Dependence on a few key data vendors.
- Underperformance in specific historical regimes.

This section requires intellectual honesty. It is better to admit limitations upfront than to pretend the model is universally robust.

7. Governance and Contacts

Finally, the card records:

- Named model owner.
- Primary researcher(s).
- Model Risk contact.
- Operational contact for production issues.

With such a card, the model ceases to be a mysterious black box. It becomes a documented object that can be debated, challenged, and improved.

Versioning: Freezing a Moving Target

Models evolve. Code is refactored, parameters are updated, vendors change data formats, and new risk controls are introduced. Without a disciplined versioning scheme, it quickly becomes impossible to answer a basic forensic question: *what exactly was running last Tuesday at 10:15 am when we lost money?*

To solve this, we need to version at least four artifacts:

- Model code.
- Configuration and parameters.
- Data snapshots used for backtesting and training.
- The model card itself.

The key idea is that any *production run*—for example, generating today's trades—can be tied to a specific bundle of these versions.

Code Versioning

Code versioning is now standard practice in software development, and quant teams should be no exception. At a minimum:

- All model-related code lives in a version-controlled repository (e.g., Git).
- Every change is committed with a descriptive message explaining what and why.
- Production deployments use tagged releases (e.g., equity_value_v1.3.2) rather than arbitrary branches or local copies.

From a model risk perspective, the important property is *reproducibility*: given a tag, you can check out exactly the same code that was live at that time.

Configuration and Parameters

Most models have parameters that can be changed without altering code: risk limits, signal weights, lookback windows, feature on/off flags, and so on. If these live in free-form spreadsheets or ad hoc text files, silent changes are almost guaranteed.

To prevent this:

- Configuration files (JSON, YAML, or similar) are treated as code: checked into the repository, versioned, and reviewed.
- Parameter sets used in production are named and tagged (e.g., config_value_v1.0, config_value_v1.1_reduced_leverage).
- Any on-the-fly override (such as lowering a risk limit manually during a stress event) is logged with operator, timestamp, and reason.

The combination of code tag and configuration tag defines a specific *model implementation*. You might refer to it in the model card or an internal registry as, say, "Equity Value, implementation 1.3.2 / config 1.1."

Data Snapshots and Training Sets

Backtests and training results are only meaningful if you know which data they were based on. Data vendors correct errors and restate fields; internal cleaning rules evolve. Without data versioning, reproduction is impossible.

Practical approaches include:

- Storing training and backtest datasets as immutable snapshots (for example, using date-stamped directories or content-addressable storage).
- Recording, for each snapshot:
- Date of extraction.
- Source systems and versions.
- Any applied cleaning or transformation scripts (also version-controlled).
- Including the data snapshot identifier in backtest reports and in the model card's validation section.

You do not need to freeze every tick of raw market data forever, but you should at least freeze the derived datasets that directly feed model development.

Versioning the Model Card

The model card itself is a living document. As assumptions change or new data sources are added, it should be updated. To keep history:

- Store the model card in text or markup format (e.g., LaTeX or Markdown) under version control.
- Tag the card with the implementation versions it describes.
- Keep a change log summarizing major updates (e.g., "v1.2: added alternative momentum feature; widened universe to include mid-caps").

This way, when you look back at a historical drawdown, you can see not only which implementation was live, but also which assumptions were officially documented at that time.

Change Control: From Tinkering to Managed Evolution

Versioning captures *what* changed. Change control governs *how* and *why* changes are made. Without it, production models are vulnerable to undocumented tweaks, unreviewed bugfixes, and parametric overfitting creeping in under the guise of "small improvements."

A sensible change control process differentiates between:

- **Minor changes**: cosmetic refactors, logging improvements, or risk-lowering config changes with no impact on core behavior.
- **Material changes**: anything that touches signal generation, risk targeting, trading logic, or capital allocation.

Change Proposals and Impact Assessment

For material changes, a lightweight "change proposal" should be drafted. It does not need to be lengthy, but it should answer:

- What is being changed?
- Why is the change needed (bug fix, performance issue, data vendor change, risk concern)?
- What is the expected impact on risk and performance?
- How has the change been tested (backtests, paper trading, shadow runs)?

This proposal is then reviewed by relevant parties: the model owner, Model Risk, and Operations. Their role is to challenge assumptions, verify that testing is adequate, and assess interactions with other models.

Before/After Comparisons

To discourage p-hacking and selective reporting, any material change should be accompanied by explicit before/after comparisons, using:

- The same historical period.

- The same transaction cost and slippage assumptions.
- The same risk limits and universe.

The goal is transparency. If the new version improves Sharpe but doubles maximum drawdown, that trade-off should be made explicit and consciously accepted (or rejected) by the approving committee.

Pre-Registration and Hypothesis Logging

In academic research, pre-registration of hypotheses is used to counter data mining. In trading, full pre-registration is often impractical, but you can move in that direction by:

- Logging high-level research hypotheses before intensive experimentation (e.g., "We believe adding a 6-month volatility feature will reduce crash sensitivity").
- Recording which hypotheses were confirmed, which were rejected, and which were inconclusive.

Over time, this log becomes a valuable record of what has been tried and how often apparent outperformance failed to survive out-of-sample tests.

Approvals, Rollbacks, and Post-Change Review

Once a change is accepted:

- The new implementation (code + config) receives a version tag and is deployed according to a runbook.
- A *rollback plan* is prepared: what conditions would trigger reversing to the previous version, and how quickly can this be done?
- An initial review window is defined (for example, "Two weeks after deployment, we will assess whether realized behavior matches expectations").

This closes the loop: changes are not only approved in advance but also evaluated after the fact.

Audit Trails and Forensic Reconstruction

When something goes wrong—a sudden loss, a strange trading pattern, or a monitoring alert—you need to reconstruct the chain of events. Without an audit trail, conversations degenerate into opinion: "It must have been the market," "We didn't change anything important," and so on.

A robust audit trail links each production run to:

- The model implementation version (code tag + config tag).
- The data snapshot or feed version used that day (where applicable).
- Any manual overrides (risk limits, trading halts, parameter changes), along with operator, timestamp, and reason.
- The set of trades submitted and fills received.

With this information, you can:

- Re-run the model on the same inputs to verify that the outputs match (isolating potential execution issues).
- Compare realized behavior with backtested expectations under similar conditions.
- Identify whether a particular code change correlates with a shift in performance.

This is crucial for separating *signal decay* (the edge genuinely eroding) from *implementation failure* (a bug or misconfiguration causing unintended trades).

Learning from Model Retirements

No model lives forever. Markets change, competition erodes edges, and some strategies simply stop working. When a model is retired, you have a choice:

- Treat it as a one-off disappointment and move on.
- Or treat it as a data point in a long-term organizational learning process.

Disciplined documentation and change control make the second option feasible. A thoughtful retirement review can answer questions such as:

- Did the model fail because its economic rationale broke down, or because assumptions about costs and liquidity became outdated?
- Were there early warning signs in monitoring that we ignored?
- Did subsequent changes (new features, more complexity) actually accelerate overfitting and decay?
- Should our standards for data quality, validation, or stress testing be tightened in light of what happened?

The model card provides the original intent and assumptions. The version history shows how the model evolved. The audit trail and monitoring records reveal how it behaved in the wild. Together, they allow you to write a rigorous "post-mortem" that improves future governance and research practice.

From Craft to Engineering Discipline

Quant trading will always have an element of craft. Insight and creativity cannot be replaced by templates. But once a model is destined for production, it must be treated as an engineered system, not a personal spreadsheet.

Model cards, version control, change proposals, and audit trails may feel like administrative overhead at first. Yet they are what allow:

- Independent teams to *understand* and *challenge* a model.
- Operators to run it safely and reconstruct its behavior.

- Organizations to tell whether a disappointing period is a statistical fluctuation, a coding error, or genuine signal decay.

In the broader arc of this book, these practices complement the technical tools for avoiding overfitting and detecting drift. Good documentation and change control do not guarantee that your models will never fail. But they ensure that failures are explainable, reversible, and, most importantly, instructive.

6.3 Post-Deployment Monitoring and Drift Alerts

In the previous sections we put in place the *front-end* defenses against model failure: clear ownership and challenge rights, careful documentation, and disciplined change control. All of that work culminates in a model being promoted to production with a well-understood set of expectations: its risk profile, its typical performance range, and the data it depends on.

Once the model is live, the problem changes. The main question is no longer “Is this backtest believable?” but rather “Is the live model still behaving like the object we approved?” Markets shift, data vendors change specifications, and small implementation bugs creep in. If you only revisit a model when a large loss hits the P&L, you are too late.

This section describes how to build a *monitoring layer* that:

- Compares live behavior to the expectations set by backtests and the model card.
- Detects *drift* in performance, behavior, and data inputs.
- Raises *actionable* alerts early enough that losses can be contained.

The emphasis is on structure and practicality. Monitoring should not be a dashboard no one looks at; it should be a process that reliably drives decisions.

Three Monitoring Lanes: Performance, Behavior, Data

A useful mental model is to think of monitoring as three parallel "lanes," each watching for a different class of deviation.

Performance Monitoring

Performance monitoring looks at the *outputs* the investment team cares about most: returns and risk. Typical key performance indicators (KPIs) include:

- Daily or weekly strategy returns.
- Rolling Sharpe ratio or information ratio.
- Hit rate (fraction of profitable trades or days).
- Realized versus targeted volatility.
- Drawdowns and time under water.

The aim is to check whether these KPIs remain within the bands implied by the backtest and stress tests. For example, if the backtest suggests that a one-month rolling Sharpe below -0.5 is extremely rare, seeing a sequence of such values in live trading is a clear warning signal.

Behavioral Monitoring

Performance alone can be misleading: a model might still be making money while quietly drifting into very different behavior. Behavioral monitoring watches the *internal mechanics* of the strategy, such as:

- Distribution of signals (e.g., how many names are strongly long, neutral, or strongly short).
- Position sizes and concentration (e.g., top 10 holdings as a percentage of gross exposure).
- Turnover and holding period distribution.
- Exposure to known risk factors (value, momentum, carry, volatility, sectors, regions).

- Trade routing patterns and use of specific venues or brokers.

The question here is: "Is the model still trading the way we think it is?" A surge in turnover, a sudden increase in factor concentration, or a collapse in the number of active positions may signal implementation issues, universe changes, or unintended consequences of a recent code/config change.

Data Monitoring

Finally, even a perfect model will fail if its inputs are corrupted. Data monitoring focuses on properties of the *input streams*:

- Basic sanity checks (e.g., prices non-negative, corporate actions applied, timestamps increasing).
- Distributional checks (e.g., mean and variance of a feature compared with historical values).
- Missingness patterns (e.g., proportion of instruments with missing signals or stale data).
- Vendor-level health (e.g., feed delays, disconnects, sudden jumps in revisions).

Data drift is insidious because it may not show up immediately in P&L, especially for diversified portfolios. Without explicit checks, you might discover months later that a vendor quietly changed its definition of a key field.

From Expectations to Control Limits

Monitoring is only effective if you know what deviations are normal. The backtest and model card provide a natural reference point. The process has three steps:

1. Quantify Historical Behavior

Using the same code and data snapshot used in validation, compute for each KPI:

- A central tendency measure (mean, median).

- A dispersion measure (standard deviation, interquartile range).
- The distribution of rolling-window statistics (e.g., 1-month Sharpe, 3-month drawdown).

Do the same for key behavioral metrics (turnover, signal dispersion, factor exposures) and for data-quality metrics (missingness rates, feature moments).

The goal is to obtain a sense of the "typical" and the "extreme but historically observed."

2. Define Control Bands

Based on historical behavior and risk appetite, define *control bands* or thresholds for each metric. For example:

- One-month rolling Sharpe: expected range $[-0.5, 1.5]$; soft alert if below -0.5, hard alert if below -1.0.
- Daily turnover: expected range $[5\%, 20\%]$ of portfolio; alert if it exceeds 30%.
- Proportion of assets with missing signals: expected below 2%; alert above 5%.

These bands should be documented, not made up on the fly. They represent a compact translation of "what we saw in the backtest and consider acceptable."

3. Calibrate to Live Noise

Reality will never match the backtest perfectly. Early in a model's life, monitor alerts may fire too frequently or not enough. It is therefore sensible to have an initial calibration phase:

- Start with conservative (wider) bands to avoid excessive false alarms.
- After a few months, review how often alerts fired and whether they were informative.
- Tighten or adjust bands, and refine which alerts require immediate action versus investigation at the next review meeting.

The crucial point is that thresholds are not arbitrary; they are anchored in historical behavior and iteratively improved.

Visualizing Backtest vs Live: A Multi-Panel View

A practical way to make drift visible is to juxtapose backtest-derived expectations with live outcomes in the same visual space. A common pattern is a three-panel chart:

- Top panel: rolling returns or Sharpe.
- Middle panel: hit rate or another performance diagnostic.
- Bottom panel: a key behavioral or signal-distribution metric.

In each panel you plot:

- A control band (for example, the 5th to 95th percentile from the backtest).
- The actual live series as it evolves.
- Markers where live values breach the control band.

This integrated view helps distinguish between different types of regimes: those where performance is poor but behavior and data are normal (possible signal decay), versus those where both behavior and data are abnormal (likely implementation or data issues).

Such charts should be generated automatically as part of the monitoring system, updated at whatever frequency is appropriate (daily for many strategies, intraday for high-frequency ones).

Implementing the Monitoring Layer

Conceptually, monitoring sits between the model and the humans who are accountable for it. Technically, it can be implemented as a separate process that:

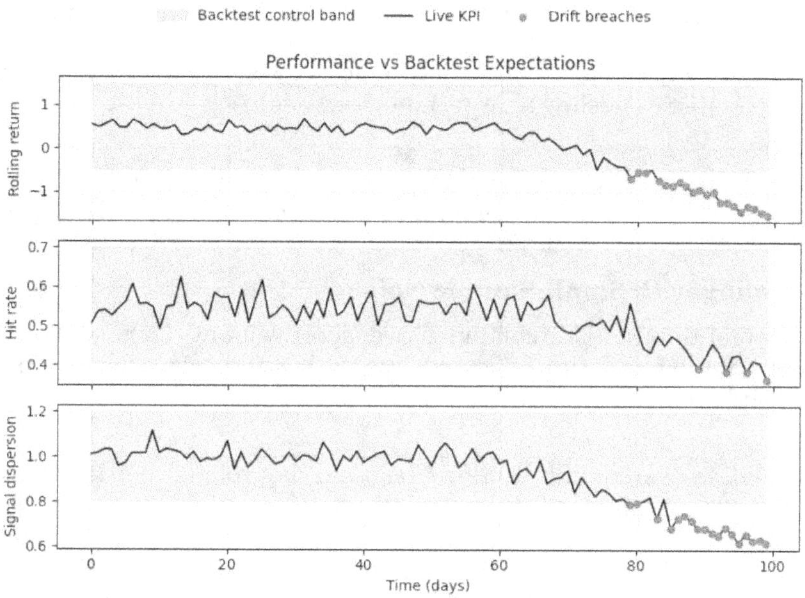

Figure 6.1: Illustrative multi-panel monitoring chart. Each panel shows a KPI with a backtest-derived control band, the live series, and red markers highlighting drift breaches.

- Ingests live outputs and inputs (signals, positions, trades, data feeds).
- Computes KPIs and checks them against control bands.
- Logs metrics and any breaches.
- Notifies relevant parties according to a predefined workflow.

Several design choices deserve attention.

Monitoring Horizons

Not all metrics need the same time resolution. For example:

- Intraday monitoring for trade-level anomalies (huge orders, repeated rejects, sudden spread widening).

- Daily monitoring for P&L, exposures, and key behavioral metrics.
- Weekly or monthly monitoring for slower-moving performance statistics (rolling Sharpe, hit rate trends).

Overly high frequency can swamp you with noise; overly low frequency can delay detection. The compromise depends on the model's horizon and risk.

Dealing with Small-Sample Noise

Any real-time statistic computed over short windows is noisy. You do not want to halt a strategy every time the last three days happen to be down. Some practical mitigants:

- Use overlapping windows (e.g., 20-day rolling metrics) rather than single-day values.
- Combine multiple indicators: a single weak signal may not trigger an alert, but a combination might (e.g., low hit rate *and* elevated drawdown).
- Distinguish *soft* alerts ("investigate at next review") from *hard* alerts ("immediate attention, possible trading halt").

Over time, you can refine rules based on which alerts proved useful and which were mostly noise.

Defining Drift and Alert Logic

"Drift" is a broad term; here we give it a concrete operational meaning. A drift event is when one or more monitored metrics moves *persistently* outside its expected band in a way that cannot be explained by random variation alone.

Common types of drift include:

- **Performance drift**: sustained underperformance or volatility far outside historical norms.

- **Behavioral drift**: significant shifts in signal distribution, turnover, or factor exposures, even if performance is temporarily fine.
- **Data drift**: changes in input distributions or missingness patterns, possibly due to vendor or pipeline changes.

Alert logic should map combinations of metric breaches to clear actions. For example:

- *Case A*: Performance metrics breach soft bands, behavior and data normal. Action: PM and Model Risk review; no immediate trading changes, but heightened monitoring.
- *Case B*: Behavior metrics breach; positions or exposures outside normal range. Action: PM and Operations investigate for bugs or config errors; potential temporary risk reduction.
- *Case C*: Data metrics breach; sudden spike in missing inputs. Action: Operations may temporarily freeze new orders from affected model until data integrity is restored.
- *Case D*: Multiple hard breaches (performance, behavior, and/or data). Action: escalate to risk committee; consider halting or materially scaling down the model.

The goal is to avoid both paralysis (no one acts) and chaos (everyone acts differently each time). A written playbook turns alerts into decisions rather than anxiety.

Alerting Workflow and Accountability

Monitoring is not just numbers; it is a social process. The workflow should answer:

- Who receives which alerts (PMs, Model Risk, Operations, senior management)?
- In what form (emails, chat messages, dashboard flags, incident tickets)?

- Who is responsible for acknowledging an alert and by when?
- Where is the response documented?

One simple pattern is:

- Soft alerts appear on dashboards and in daily reports; discussed in regular model review meetings.
- Hard alerts create incident tickets assigned to the model owner, with Model Risk copied.
- For the most severe alerts, paging or immediate chat messages may be appropriate.

Crucially, each alert should result in a short, dated note: what was investigated, what was concluded, and whether any actions were taken. This builds a history that helps calibrate future thresholds and provides context in later post-mortems.

Monitoring as an Antidote to Silent Signal Decay

In the context of this book, monitoring is a primary defense against *silent* signal decay—the slow erosion of edge that goes unnoticed until a crisis. It helps in several ways:

- **Early detection**: Performance drift relative to backtest expectations surfaces quickly, prompting investigation before losses compound.
- **Root cause separation**: By jointly watching performance, behavior, and data, you can often distinguish economic decay (performance only) from implementation or data issues (behavior/-data anomalies).
- **Feedback into research**: Persistent drift patterns (e.g., signal dispersion shrinking across many models) can inform research about structural market changes.

- **Support for champion–challenger**: Monitoring provides the evidence base for later decisions about when to demote a champion model or promote a challenger, a topic we address in the next section.

Monitoring does not prevent all model failures. But it changes their character: instead of being surprised by a sudden blow-up, you see a traceable path of warning signs and responses.

From One-Off Checks to an Operating Rhythm

The last conceptual shift is cultural. Monitoring must not be a one-off checklist item during go-live; it should become part of the daily and weekly rhythm of the organization:

- Model owners review dashboards daily and acknowledge any new hard alerts.
- Model Risk runs periodic (e.g., monthly) monitoring reviews across families of models, looking for shared drift patterns.
- Operations track data and execution metrics continuously, ensuring technical health.
- Senior risk committees periodically review summarized monitoring results and incident histories.

When monitoring is integrated into routine decision-making, it stops being an afterthought and becomes a core component of the model lifecycle. Combined with the governance, documentation, and change control practices developed earlier, it allows a trading organization to live with the reality of overfitting and signal decay—not by denying them, but by detecting and managing them early, before they turn into existential threats.

6.4 Champion-Challenger and Refresh Policies

In the previous section we built a monitoring layer that continuously compares live behavior with backtests, detects drift, and raises alerts. Monitoring tells you *that* something has changed; it does not, by itself, tell you what to do next. This section focuses on the decision layer that sits on top of monitoring: a structured way to refresh, replace, or retire models.

The central idea is to stop treating any model as permanent. Instead, every live model is a *champion* that holds its place only as long as it remains competitive against *challengers*. Signal decay is treated as a fact of life, not a surprise. The organization's default stance is: "This model works for now, but we are continuously testing alternatives and will replace it when the evidence shifts."

We will:

- Define champion and challenger roles and how they are run in practice.
- Explain fair comparison rules so that results are statistically and operationally meaningful.
- Describe refresh and retirement policies: when to promote, demote, or decommission a model.
- Address model proliferation and complexity control.
- Connect these ideas to the broader lifecycle of research, monitoring, and governance.

Champion and Challenger: Roles and Intuition

At any point in time, for a given trading problem (for example, "medium-horizon equity value" or "intraday futures spread"), you designate:

- A **champion**: the current production model that carries most or all of the capital for that problem.
- One or more **challengers**: alternative specifications, refreshed calibrations, or entirely new models that are being tested against the champion.

The champion is not assumed to be "the best" in any absolute sense; it is simply "the best we are currently willing to trust with real capital." Challengers exist to provide continual pressure: they represent the next generation, and they are given a structured path to promotion if they demonstrate superior and robust performance.

This approach has three major benefits:

- It forces the research pipeline to remain active and connected to production decisions.
- It reduces the emotional attachment to any single model; everything is provisional.
- It gives you a disciplined way to respond to signal decay detected in monitoring.

How to Run Challengers: Shadow and Limited-Capital Modes

A challenger can be run in two main modes, depending on the maturity of the idea and the organization's risk appetite.

Shadow Mode

In *shadow mode*, the challenger:

- Receives the same inputs as the champion (data, tradable universe, constraints).
- Produces signals, positions, and hypothetical trades on the same schedule.
- Is not allowed to send real orders; it is evaluated on *paper* P&L using realistic simulations of execution and costs.

Shadow mode is most suitable for:

- Early testing of a new architecture or feature set.
- Risky or more complex models where confidence is low.
- Models that would materially change portfolio characteristics if fully deployed.

The advantage of shadow mode is safety: you can accumulate evidence without risking capital. The cost is that simulated execution and costs, no matter how carefully modeled, may differ from reality.

Limited-Capital Mode

In *limited-capital mode*, the challenger is allowed to trade real capital, but with explicit constraints:

- A small fraction of the capital currently allocated to the champion (for example, 5–20%).
- Possibly tighter risk limits (max position size, gross and net exposure, leverage).
- In some setups, the challenger may trade in a segregated sub-portfolio for clean attribution.

Limited-capital mode is appropriate when:

- The challenger has already passed strict backtests and shadow tests.
- Operational and data pipelines have been validated.
- Management is willing to accept some risk in exchange for more realistic evaluation.

Running real capital through a challenger has two benefits. First, it reveals any real-world frictions or execution issues that paper tests missed. Second, it forces the team to confront trade-offs: capital allocated to the challenger is capital not allocated to the champion.

Fair Comparison Rules

For the champion-challenger framework to be credible, comparisons must be *fair*. Otherwise, results can be gamed and decisions will be driven by noise or by artifacts of differing assumptions.

Key principles include:

Same Execution Assumptions

When comparing live or shadow P&L:

- Use the same transaction cost and slippage models for both champion and challenger when computing paper P&L.
- If both trade live, normalize for differences in broker fees, liquidity tiers, or explicit constraints.

A model that appears superior only because it assumes unrealistically low costs is not a true challenger; it is just mis-specified.

Comparable Risk and Capital

You should aim, as far as practical, to compare models at similar risk levels:

- Target similar volatility or risk budgets for champion and challenger.
- Compare returns on a risk-adjusted basis (e.g., Sharpe or information ratio).
- Where constraints differ, disclose and, if needed, re-scale P&L to a common risk target.

Otherwise, a challenger that simply takes more risk may look better in raw returns but be unacceptable from a risk standpoint.

Consistent Evaluation Windows

Performance should be evaluated over pre-agreed windows:

- For medium-horizon strategies, this might mean at least 6–12 months of live or shadow data.

- For faster strategies, shorter windows may suffice, but they must still aggregate enough trades to have statistical meaning.

Crucially, these windows should be specified *before* the comparison, not cherry-picked ex post from periods where the challenger looks best.

Multiple Metrics, Not Just Sharpe

Decisions should not be based on a single metric. In addition to risk-adjusted returns, consider:

- Maximum drawdown and tail risk.
- Stability of factor exposures and correlations with other models.
- Capacity and scalability (how much capital each model can absorb).
- Operational complexity and fragility (number of dependencies, sensitivity to data quirks).

A challenger that delivers a modest Sharpe improvement but introduces substantially more complexity or tail risk may not be worth promoting.

Refresh and Retirement Policies

With fair comparisons in place, you can now define rules that govern when the champion holds its seat, when a challenger is promoted, and when a model is retired entirely. These rules should be documented in governance policies, not improvised ad hoc.

Promotion Criteria: When Does a Challenger Win?

Promotion criteria specify what evidence is needed to replace or augment the champion. Typical ingredients include:

- **Performance gates**: The challenger exceeds the champion's risk-adjusted return by a specified margin (for example, a higher rolling Sharpe by at least a certain amount) over a minimum evaluation period.

- **Risk and behavior checks**: The challenger's drawdowns, factor exposures, and behavioral metrics remain within acceptable bounds and, ideally, compare favorably with the champion.
- **Robustness and stability**: Results are not driven by a few isolated events; performance is reasonably consistent across subperiods and market regimes in the evaluation window.
- **Operational readiness**: Data and execution pipelines have proven stable in shadow or limited-capital mode; no unresolved incident patterns.

Promotion need not be all-or-nothing. You might:

- Gradually shift capital from champion to challenger as confidence builds.
- Run both in production with complementary allocations if they diversify each other.
- Merge concepts: incorporate parts of the challenger's logic into the champion's new version, subject to full change-control and validation.

Demotion and Retirement Criteria for the Champion

Monitoring provides a stream of information about champions. Refresh policies translate that into actions. Demotion or retirement triggers typically include:

- **Persistent performance drift**: For example, the champion's rolling Sharpe falling below a documented minimum threshold for a sustained period (such as three or six months), taking into account expected variability.
- **Unacceptable drawdowns or tail events**: Exceeding predefined drawdown or Value-at-Risk limits, especially if monitoring shows the behavior is not aligned with the model's documented assumptions.

- **Structural breaks**: Evidence from monitoring and research that the model's economic rationale has been undermined (e.g., changes in regulation, market microstructure, or competition).
- **Operational fragility**: Repeated incidents related to data, execution, or implementation that indicate the model is too complex or brittle relative to its edge.

Responses can be tiered:

- *Soft refresh*: Reduce capital, tighten risk limits, increase challenger capital, and initiate a research review.
- *Hard demotion*: Remove the model from its role as champion; either replace it with a challenger or move to a simpler baseline model.
- *Retirement*: Fully decommission the model, preserving documentation and post-mortem analysis for future learning.

These actions should follow pre-agreed playbooks to avoid paralysis or emotionally driven decisions in the midst of drawdowns.

Minimum Live-Test Durations

To avoid overreacting to noise, it is often wise to specify minimum live-test durations:

- A challenger must run for at least a certain number of trades or months before it can be promoted, unless there is overwhelming evidence.
- Similarly, a champion is not demoted based on the first bad week, unless limits are breached in extreme fashion.

These rules encourage patience where appropriate but do not block decisive action when thresholds are clearly crossed.

Managing Model Proliferation and Complexity

Champion-challenger frameworks can, if mismanaged, lead to ever-growing sets of lightly used models: many challengers, few decisive decisions. That increases operational risk and cognitive load. To prevent this, policies should address:

Caps on Concurrent Challengers

For each trading problem or asset class, you can set a maximum number of active challengers (for example, two or three at a time). When the limit is reached:

- New contenders must first prove themselves in pure research or offline tests.
- An underperforming or stalled challenger may need to be retired to make room.

This forces prioritization and keeps the evaluation effort focused.

Periodic Pruning

On a fixed schedule (say, quarterly), conduct a *challenger review*:

- Assess each challenger against predefined performance and learning objectives.
- Retire challengers that have clearly failed to add value or to produce useful insights.
- Decide whether to promote, downsize, or leave unchanged.

A challenger that did not "win" can still be valuable if it clarified that certain ideas do not work in current markets. The key is to document the findings and simplify the live model set.

Complexity Budgets

To keep the overall system comprehensible, some firms impose a *complexity budget*:

- Limit the total number of distinct production models.

- Prefer promoting challengers that simplify the stack (for example, replacing three overlapping niche models with one broader, better-structured model).
- Penalize excessive dependencies or fragile architectures when evaluating challengers.

This helps ensure that the model library remains explainable and maintainable, not an unmanageable zoo.

Integrating Champion-Challenger with Governance and Monitoring

The champion-challenger mechanism is not an isolated gadget; it interacts tightly with the governance and monitoring layers you already established:

- **Ownership**: Each champion and challenger has a named model owner responsible for monitoring and decisions about promotions or retirements.
- **Model Risk**: The validation function reviews not only initial deployment but also the evidence used to justify promotions and demotions, checking that comparisons are fair and thresholds are respected.
- **Documentation**: Model cards for champions and challengers record their intended roles, assumptions, and validation history. When a challenger is promoted, its card and version history become the new reference.
- **Monitoring**: The same monitoring infrastructure tracks KPIs, behavior, and data for both champions and challengers, enabling side-by-side comparisons over consistent windows.
- **Change Control**: Promotion or demotion of a model is itself a material change. It follows the same approval workflow as any major modification, including impact assessment and rollback plans.

In effect, the champion-challenger framework operationalizes the idea that models are *versioned, reviewable products*, not one-off research projects.

Accepting Decay, Institutionalizing Renewal

Taken together, champion-challenger and refresh policies amount to institutionalizing humility. Instead of assuming that clever models will keep working indefinitely, you:

- Assume that edges will decay as markets adapt and competitors learn.
- Continuously test new ideas against current champions in a disciplined, controlled manner.
- Use monitoring signals not as verdicts but as prompts to adjust capital, promote challengers, or retire stale approaches.

This mindset has a subtle but powerful effect on culture. Researchers know that their models will face ongoing competition and scrutiny; PMs know that poor performance will lead to structured review rather than ad hoc blame; risk managers have transparent criteria for escalating concerns.

In a field where overfitting and signal decay are unavoidable, such a framework does not eliminate failure. It does something more realistic and more valuable: it makes failure *manageable*, *explainable*, and *reversible*. Models are born, mature, age, and eventually retire-but within a lifecycle that is understood and actively managed, rather than left to chance.

www.ingramcontent.com/pod-product-compliance
Lightning Source LLC
LaVergne TN
LVHW022156200926
848481LV00006B/1763
* 9 7 9 8 8 9 6 6 5 2 3 3 5 *